# TAKING

## Motherhood

# TO HEARTS

*a guide to* **STARTING,**
**LEADING,** *and* **TENDING**
*your* **MOM HEART GROUP**

# Taking Motherhood to Hearts

A Guide to Starting,
Leading, and Tending
Your Mom Heart Group

A motherhood ministry initiative of
**Whole Heart Ministries**

**Taking Motherhood to Hearts**
Published by Whole Heart Press
A division of Whole Heart Ministries
P.O. Box 3445, Monument, CO 80132
WholeHeart.org • MomHeart.com

© 2014 Whole Heart Ministries
ISBN: 978-1-888692-27-3

First Edition: January 2015

Unless otherwise indicated, all Scripture verses are taken from the New American Standard Bible®. Copyright ©1960, 1962, 1963, 1968, 1971, 1972, 1973, 1975, 1977, 1995 by The Lockman Foundation. Used by permission. (www.Lockman.org)

Scripture quotations marked NIV are taken from the HOLY BIBLE, NEW INTER-NATIONAL VERSION®. NIV®. Copyright © 1973, 1978, 1984 by International Bible Society. Used by permission of Zondervan. All rights reserved. (www.Zondervan.com).

Scripture quotations marked NET are taken from the NET Bible®. Copyright ©1996-2006 by Biblical Studies Press, L.L.C. Used by permission. All rights reserved. (www.Bible.org)

Mom Heart Ministry is a motherhood initiative of Whole Heart Ministries, a Christian home and parenting ministry dedicated since 1994 to encouraging and equipping Christian parents to raise wholehearted Christian children.

# Table of Contents

## Section 4: The Ministry

## Section 5: The Model

## Section 6: The Mentor

## Section 7: The Mission

# A Note from Sally Clarkson
# WELCOME TO MOM HEART!

**Dear Sweet Mom,**

Thank you for your interest in ministering to mothers. My own mom heart beats with a passion to encourage mothers and to help them rediscover God's heart for motherhood. *Taking Motherhood to Hearts*, along with your Bible and our other materials and resources, will equip you to start, lead, and tend a Mom Heart group of your own in your community or church.

Time is precious, especially for moms. If you give a few hours of your week to something, you want it to be purposeful and meaningful. The heart of our ministry is to encourage, equip, and enable you as a mother with a heart for ministry. We'll help you have an effective ministry that "redeems the time" for God.

All of my Mom Heart leaders are praying for you. We are working on ways to stay connected with you and to support you in your ministry. You are not alone. You are part of a growing movement of small groups that are taking motherhood to hearts. I believe God's Spirit is raising up moms like you "for such a time as this."

I hope you will join me, and so many other mothers already involved, as we step out in faith to build a community of Mom Heart moms all over the world. Help us restore moms' hearts to God's heart for motherhood "that the generation to come might know, even the children yet to be born" (Psalm 78:6).

**In His Heart,**

# Section 1
# THE MOVEMENT

**History is shaped by movements.** Like powerful rivers, ideas at the right time can flow through history for good or for evil, cutting through what once seemed solid and changing the landscape of cultures for generations to come. You can become part of a movement for good by starting and leading a Mom Heart group. You can join with many other moms to change hearts, change families, and even change the landscape of eternity. Get in the flow of a movement of moms bringing the river of life into wherever they are. The time is right to make a difference.

The fundamental mission of motherhood now is the same as it always was: to nurture, protect, and instruct children, to create a home environment that enables them to learn and grow, to help them develop a heart for God and his purposes, and to send them out into the world prepared to live both fully and meaningfully.

*~ The Mission of Motherhood,* Sally Clarkson

# Seeing the "Big Picture" of Mom Heart

We live in a rapidly secularizing culture that is losing its heart for biblical motherhood. As the sacred institution of marriage has grown steadily weaker over the past few generations, American culture has largely abandoned any notion it once held that child bearing, arguably the highest purpose of marriage, is a sacred calling. If God is in the cultural picture at all, he is often little more than a divine bystander.

Feminism has produced generations of young women who, because they have not been taught or trained about the biblical design for motherhood, view motherhood simply as one of many goals and tasks that the modern woman must learn how to manage efficiently. It is not seen as a divine calling, a strategic part of God's eternal plan for transmitting faith through generations of families. Rather, it has become merely another option to consider, or just one of the many commitments in a modern woman's life. Many Christian mothers can even find themselves subtly conforming, willingly or unwillingly, to the prevailing culture. As the cultural understanding of what it means to be a mother evolves, it appears that traditional, biblical motherhood is increasingly marginalized and even minimalized.

The high calling of biblical motherhood is being swept away in a tidal wave of societal change, pushed aside by a secularized culture that no longer values God's view of family, home, and motherhood. The once dominant idea that a mother at home with her children is normative and desirable has been run off the road by the fast moving traffic of postmodern life. It gets passed by like an older model car that no one really drives anymore that can't keep up with the pace of life in the twenty-first century.

> The time is right to renew and revive mothers' vision for biblical motherhood. Mothers are a strategic, open, waiting, and under-served mission field.

Many young women who are marrying and having children now often have grown up with little or no direct influence by strong models of Christian motherhood. Even if they have close and loving relationships with their mothers, they often lack any biblical training at home, or from the church or Christian community, about what it means to have God's heart for motherhood. They have not rejected a biblical, traditional model of motherhood; they simply don't know what it is.

For over two decades, Sally Clarkson has called mothers back to God's design, driven by her personal passion to restore moms' hearts to God's heart for motherhood. As a seasoned mother of four children, she has championed God's biblical design for the family, and especially for motherhood. Her heart beats for Titus 2:3-5 motherhood and for 2 Timothy 2:2 discipleship as she comes alongside Christian moms to give voice and value to God's biblical principles and priorities of motherhood.

Though the wider culture in which we live often either dismisses as outdated or openly disdains biblical ideals for motherhood, Sally holds them up and points moms back to them. Her vision for Mom Heart Ministry is to catalyze a movement of small groups of mothers around the world that will leave an indelible, eternal imprint on the next generation for Christ and His kingdom.

The time is right to renew and revive mothers' vision for biblical motherhood. Mothers are a strategic, open, waiting, and under-served mission field. But more than that, they are a spiritual force waiting to be unleashed on a coming generation of Christ followers being raised in their homes. Mom Heart Ministry wants to bring those ministry-minded moms together to make a difference.

## Where Do You Fit in the Picture of Mom Heart?

Motherhood is more than just a biblical duty. It is a ministry of discipleship. Before he departed to be with the Father, Jesus gave us one great command: "Make disciples!" That is our mission in our time on this earth—to make followers of Jesus.

But that mission actually began in the beginning of creation, in the book of Genesis. Before Adam and Eve fell into sin, God created them and gave them the mandate to "fill the earth." Implicit in that mission was the understanding that those who filled the earth would then follow the Creator. In other words, making children was God's original plan for making disciples. But then there was the fall.

We live now in a broken world. God's design and plan for family has been distorted, but it has not changed. Our highest calling as Christian parents is to "make disciples" of our children—to "bring them up in the discipline and instruction of the Lord" (Ephesians 6:4) so they will follow Christ and build His kingdom in their generation, and to "teach them diligently" (Deuteronomy 6:7) to love God with all their "heart, soul, mind, and strength" (Mark 12:30, Luke 10:27).

By nature and by nurture, mothers are inextricably part of that discipleship process. God's design for home and family places moms at the center of influence in their children's lives. Mothers are, in many ways, the heart of parenting.

Our vision for Mom Heart Ministry is to restore moms' hearts to God's heart for motherhood. We want to offer God's grace and truth from His Word that will set them free, not weigh them down. We want moms to live by faith, not by formula. We want to strengthen moms who are seeking after God's heart—to help them disciple their children to become wholehearted followers of Jesus Christ, and to reach out to other mothers to impact the next generation for Him. Moms can make a difference. You can make a difference.

## Picturing the Possibilities of a Mom Heart Group

Christian ministry is not a complicated idea. The meaning of the word in the New Testament is simply "service." Ministry is how we serve God, and serve others (John 12:26; Matthew 22:34-40). There are two broad types of ministry in the New Testament: church ministry and personal ministry.

Church ministry is how God's people come together as Christ's body to worship Him, teach and preach the Word of God, and equip one another for service. Personal ministry is how each spiritually-gifted individual serves God and His kingdom to build up the body of Christ and spread the gospel. When Paul described the ministry God has given to us as Christians, he said we are all "ambassadors for Christ," and that

God is making His appeal to others through us, on behalf of Christ, that they be reconciled to God. In other words, if we are "in Christ" then we are in ministry (see: 2 Corinthians 5:17-20)

If the idea of "reconciliation" sounds like something that is above your spiritual pay grade, try substituting the phrase "coming home." Reconciliation is simply showing others the way to come home to where God always intended them to be. A Mom Heart group is one way you can be an ambassador for Christ by showing other moms how to come home to God's heart for motherhood.

> A Mom Heart group is one way you can be an ambassador for Christ by showing other moms how to come home to God's heart for motherhood.

Your Mom Heart group could be part of a church ministry, or it could be a personal ministry you offer in your community. You don't need any special gifting or training; you simply need the willingness to start, lead, and tend a small group of moms intent on hearing from God. Your personal ministry to those moms will be the catalyst that facilitates God's ministry of reconciliation by the Spirit—restoring moms' hearts to God's heart for motherhood.

The beauty of reconciliation ministry is that there is not just one way to offer it, but countless possibilities. Since we began Mom Heart Ministry in 2008, we have watched as the Spirit of God has worked through hundreds of groups in dozens of different ways. There is no "one size fits all" program for a Mom Heart group, but rather an "all sizes fit one" purpose. That one purpose is to reconcile moms to God's design for motherhood.

If you can picture yourself leading a small group of mothers, what you picture in all likelihood will look different from what others might picture in their minds. That's good. The Spirit of God creates a diversity of ministries, and gives us freedom to minister according to our own gifts and callings. Your own experiences, drives, convictions, needs, training, vision, and circumstances means that you will create a different kind of group from other mothers you know. For instance, the list below describes just a few of the many ways we have seen or contemplated Mom Heart groups being expressed:

- As a support group for friends who are mothers
- As an outreach to moms in a neighborhood
- As a group to prepare young women for motherhood
- As a support group during a mom's day out program
- As a group model for a MOPS® program
- As a groups ministry outreach to military mothers
- As a Titus 2 group to encourage younger mothers
- As an outreach and ministry to single mothers
- As a church ministry to equip mothers spiritually
- As an outreach to homeless moms
- As an outreach to at-risk teen or single moms
- As a support group for homeschooling mothers
- As a support group for public schooling mothers
- As a group to support missionary mothers
- As a group to minister to pregnant unmarried girls
- As a group to pray for mothers around the world
- As a Crisis Pregnancy Center support group
- As a mothers of prodigals support group
- As a support group for mothers of teens

- As a mother-daughter motherhood study group
- As a support group for minority moms
- As a mothers of mothers support group

Our heart and vision is to trust the Spirit of God to create a movement of Mom Heart groups all around the world that is reaching and reconciling women to the Creator and to His design for mothers. Movement is the operative word of our vision—we have no desire to create, command, and control a Mom Heart organization, but rather to facilitate and shepherd a Mom Heart movement led by the Holy Spirit. Our role is to feed that movement to keep it growing.

A healthy movement requires two key elements: a mission and a message. It needs a shared vision and a common set of core beliefs. That's why we ask every Mom Heart group leader to understand and agree with the Mom Heart Vision and Values Covenant and the Mom Heart Statement of Beliefs (see: Section 10). We want to allow freedom for every Mom Heart group to be unique in its local expression, and yet also insure that it will be consistent with other Mom Heart groups around the world. We have carefully defined the mission and message of Mom Heart Ministry for one reason: to be able to encourage as many moms as possible to come home to God's heart for motherhood.

We trust the Holy Spirit to protect the vision and values of Mom Heart Ministry, and we trust Mom Heart group leaders to creatively express them through their own unique gifts, skills, ministry burdens, training, and circumstances. Our hope and prayer is that this group leader guide will encourage, equip, and enable you, by faith, to start, lead, and tend a Mom Heart group in your part of God's world.

## Mom Heart Keeps the Picture in Focus

We know that a movement cannot exist long without an idea, person, or cause providing a stabilizing focus. Followers need something or someone to follow. Mom Heart Ministry is a cause-driven movement—we are driven by our burden to restore biblical motherhood.

However, even great ideas can become volatile and unstable in the heat of debate, and good people can become uncertain and unpredictable in the throes of life. History is strewn with movements that have come and gone, as well changed by movements that have stayed the course. We believe that a well-defined and supported biblical cause can become a stabilizing and unifying identity that creates a secure common ground for followers. Focus builds faith.

> Mom Heart Ministry is a cause-driven movement—we are driven by our burden to restore biblical motherhood.

To keep the vision of this ministry in focus, we will connect with mothers who share our heart for motherhood. We will encourage and equip mothers online with training helps, events information, blog articles, selected books and resources, webinars, social media, and more. We want to be where the new generation of mothers will be.

As we move forward, we will offer new and helpful materials and resources by Sally and other leaders, including ebooks on a variety of topics, book and topical group study guides, audio messages and podcasts, video messages, and other helpful print books and materials. We will encourage moms personally in a hotel retreat setting through our Mom Heart Conferences.

As a family-run ministry, we believe in the vision and the cause God has kept on our hearts and is expressing in Mom Heart Ministry. This group leader guide will help you start, lead, and tend a Mom Heart group as we work to encourage, equip, and enable you as a mom. As long as God allows, we will keep the ministry vision in focus that a movement of Christian moms in our brief sojourn on this earth can make an impact on eternity through the lives of mothers and their children.

# Section 2
# THE MEMBERS

**Life is not meant to be done alone.** We need others, and they need us. The apostle Paul pictured that truth for the church as a body: "For the body is not one member, but many" (1 Corinthians 12:12f). We can exist alone, but until we do life with others we can't see the beauty of the many members of the body working as one. Moms need other mothers in their lives to experience that beauty. The members of your Mom Heart group are members of your small body of friends. You bring the beauty of body life to one another.

It's easier sometimes to tell myself, "We do our devotions, we go to church, they memorize Scripture. That's all they need. I do enough." But it's not enough. What they really need is my life, my heart, my touch, my love, my patience, my correction, my gentleness, and my encouragement. They need me to be there during the many teachable moments of each day, transforming them into discipling moments because of my spiritual intent for their lives.

*~Seasons of a Mother's Heart,* Sally Clarkson

# STARTING YOUR MOM HEART GROUP

T he hardest part of doing anything worth doing is the starting. Taking that first step takes a lot of effort and energy. In physics, that idea is expressed as inertia–the tendency of a physical object to resist acceleration. In other words, left on their own, things tend to stay as they are. Unless something moves them, they don't move.

It's easy to see how this principle from physical life illustrates a similar reality in our spiritual life. We can experience spiritual inertia. If we are resistant to change–if fear, lack of confidence, insecurity, or any number of conflicting feelings keep us from moving forward–we will resist taking a first step of faith. We need some outside force to move us so we'll get moving.

But God is inertia-adverse. If you are reasonably mature, ready and willing to lead a group, but resisting the idea, you need to know that God is ready to help you move. He is ready to encourage and strengthen you to take that step of faith.

To start something new, you must overcome spiritual inertia. Something has to move you to get moving. You've probably heard it many times before, but it is true: God can't steer a parked car. If you are hesitating to take that first step of faith, know first of all that God is ready to step into your life to help. He knows you, believes in you, and wants you to lead this group, so you can trust Him to help. He won't step in until you step out in faith, but when you decide to shift out of Park and put your life in Forward, He will begin to steer. His Spirit will begin to direct you forward.

And just a reminder: The size of your group does not matter to God. He is looking for faithfulness. Every mom in your group will be special to God, whether there are two, twenty, or two hundred. Whether they are there for fellowship, for encouragement, or to learn for the first time what God says about mothering, they will be there because *God* wants them to be there. And you will be there because He wants *you* to be there for them, leading those women in seeking after God's heart as mothers.

> Every mom in your group will be special to God. They will be there because God wants them to be there.

If you are ready to step out in faith to start a Mom Heart group, there are some first steps you can take to get moving: Pray, Purpose, Plan, Partner, and Promote. If you're overcoming spiritual inertia, consider these a one-step-at-a-time way forward. These few small steps will add up to one big step of faith.

## PRAY: Ask God for Help

The first step in starting a group is to pray. You need to invite God into the process, seeking His direction and trusting Him to help you be a faithful servant to the moms He will bring to you. Following are just a few areas of prayer to consider:

- **For wisdom and discernment** – A Mom Heart group is a spiritual ministry, so your first impulse should be to pray. Don't try to start God's work without your work of prayer. Ask God for wisdom and discernment as you prepare to take a step of faith with Him. Ask for the power of the Holy Spirit in your life and in the lives of those who join you. Before you start working on a "To Do" list, set aside a morning to read Scripture, meditate on it, and listen to what God is saying to you about ministering to moms. Talk to God before you talk to others.

- **For God to provide members** – Ask God to show you who to invite to your group. Pray about mothers in your neighborhood and church who might need a group with other moms. Make a list of the women God puts on your heart, and pray for each of them regularly. If your vision and burden is for a larger group of women, such as in your church, or even for a ministry of multiple groups, pray for wisdom, resources, partners, facility, and whatever else will be needed. Always keep in mind, though, that you're praying for and about people, not just about a class or a program. Moms are the heartbeat of a Mom Heart group.

- **For mothers' hearts** – Remember that your group, whatever size it may be, is about discipleship and mutual accountability. Though fellowship is biblical and important, the reason you meet as a Mom Heart group is not just for a way to get away from home, or to have a regular coffee break and time with friends. Pray that God works in each mom's heart, including yours, to be open to what the Holy Spirit would have you learn together as moms who are seeking after God's heart. Ask God to help you respond graciously to those who are not yet interested, since they may just need time and may be future members. Pray for unity of mind and spirit, and a community of love and support.

- **For a ministry partner** – Ask God to provide a kindred spirit to be your partner in this ministry to mothers, whether as a co-leader, prayer partner, or supportive friend. Pray that God will prepare her to respond positively to your invitation to join you in this ministry. Ask her, and others, to pray for you as you seek God's direction for the group. If you envision a larger group, pray for a committed ministry team of mothers to join you in your vision.

## PURPOSE: Clarify Your Vision

Before you make a plan for your group, you need to know your purpose. Making a plan without a purpose is like trying to follow a recipe without a description of what you're cooking. Your ministry plan will be about the "who, what, when, where, and how," but your purpose will be about the "why." Having a purpose for your group may sound a bit lofty and subjective, but it is really quite simple. It is what you see with the eyes of your heart when you think about your group; it is what you picture in your mind that you want to see happen.

Proverbs 16:9 says, "The mind of man plans his way, but the LORD directs his steps." A purpose or vision statement will not only help you be able to tell others about your group, but will also help you make decisions about the group—directing you which way to go, and protecting you from going the wrong way. A good purpose or vision statement is not about plan details (who, what, when, where, how), but about the why—why should, or does, this group exist? It expresses your raison d'etre—your group's unique reason for being.

Writing a purpose statement can be a very positive and motivating exercise, even if you don't consider yourself a natural writer. Take some time to craft a statement that expresses what is really on your heart to do with your Mom Heart group. Describe what God has put on your heart. Here are a few examples you can use to get you started on your own purpose or vision statement:

- *The mission of this Mom Heart at Home group is to encourage, equip, and enable one another in the Lord as mothers after God's heart.*

- *We will meet as a Mom Heart group to give one another help and hope as mothers as we follow God's call to raise godly children for His glory.*

- *The Castle Pines Mom Heart group exists to encourage and strengthen young mothers through studying the Word of God, discussion, accountability, and fellowship.*

- *The purpose of the Grace Church Mom Heart ministry is to restore moms' hearts to God's heart for motherhood through mutual teaching, sharing, helping, and outreach.*

- *The One Heart Mom Heart Group is a safe shelter for single mothers to talk, share, learn, help, and grow as moms without partners in raising godly children.*

## PLAN: Create Your Ministry Map

Once your purpose statement is finalized, then you need to make a plan for how to accomplish that purpose. Moses was getting swamped by responsibilities of leading Israel until his father-in-law Jethro came up with a better plan. Nehemiah's well-crafted plan won Israel's release from Babylon to go back and rebuild Jerusalem. Plans help to accomplish purposes, but a good plan will be more than just a "Get It Done" list; it will be a map that expresses clearly and concisely where you want to go and how you intend to get there. Use the Mom Heart Ministry Action Plan form (see: Section 10) to help you create a MAP for your group. A thoughtful plan is an itinerary for the journey that you are about to begin, so plan to make a good plan. Here are some planning points you'll need to think about:

> Plans help to accomplish purposes, but a good plan will be more than just a "Get It Done" list; it will be a map that expresses clearly and concisely where you want to go and how you intend to get there.

- **Define the Membership** – Make a list of prospective group members. Will you focus on a certain life-stage of motherhood (new moms, moms of preschoolers, moms of teens, single moms, military moms, etc.), or will your group be open to all ages and stages of mothers? However you decide to define your membership will also affect the focus and dynamic of the group.

- **Determine the Size** – There is a certain amount of uncertainty when you first start a group. If you want it to be a home group, you will need to limit your membership size, which will limit response. A larger group will require larger facility space, more leadership, and additional resources. Know what your comfort level is for the size of your group.

- **Decide the Details** – Determine what a prospective member will need to know, such as day, meeting time, length of the meeting, frequency of meetings, location, size of group, and the material you plan to study. Anticipate questions and be ready to describe your group: "We'll meet each week for Bible study and fellowship at my house from ten o'clock until noon. We want to encourage each other as moms."

- **Consider Distractions** – Anticipate issues and consider how to prevent unnecessary distractions. Will your group be open to any moms, or will it be by invitation only? Will it be a continuing group, or new after each book or semester? Can prospective new members join in the middle of a study? Will you offer childcare and, if you do, will there be a cost?

- **Create a Calendar** – Create a projected calendar of meetings for the entire book or Bible study, with chapter to read and discuss, materials and supplies needed, possible volunteers needed, and expectations of the group such as reading a chapter or doing a study before the group. A calendar will help to engender confidence in you as a leader, and give the group as a whole a sense of direction and unity.

## PARTNER: Enlist an Ally

Paul thanked the Philippian Christians for their partnership, or fellowship (*koinonia*), in the gospel with him and expressed his love for them and his expectation of their spiritual fruitfulness (see: Philippians 1:3-11). Their partnership with him in the ministry for Christ brought Paul great joy. His calling to take the gospel to the Gentiles required him to travel thousands of miles, and on most of his journeys Paul took along companions who would learn from him, but who also would encourage him. Paul knew he needed allies for his journey of ministry, and he valued the fellowship and partnership of other believers in that work.

> Look for an ally you can pray with, be encouraged by, ask for wisdom and insight when it is needed, depend upon, and just enjoy.

Don't try to lead a group alone—you need a partner! The best time to approach another mom is when you are starting the group. Look for a mom who shares your heart for mothers, and who would be willing to assist you in leading the group. Be like Paul, though, and be open to engaging a mom who could be open to your influence. Consider this an opportunity to identify an ally who might also become an apprentice— someone you can train and encourage to start and lead their own group in the future.

Look for an ally you can pray with, be encouraged by, ask for wisdom and insight when it is needed, depend upon, and just enjoy. Ask God to lead you to the right person. Even if you plan to lead a larger group of moms with a leadership team, have an ally or two who will be your inner circle of support and encouragement.

Remember, you're not just looking for a volunteer worker, but for a valued ally. Look for these qualities in a good ministry partner:

- **Like-minded** – You share common vision and values for life and ministry.
- **Faithful** – She will be true to the purpose and plans of the group.
- **Available** – She is ready and eager to serve the needs of

other moms.

- **Teachable** – She is humble, gracious, and willing to learn and follow.
- **Reliable** – You can depend on her to do what she says she will do.

## PROMOTE: Spread the Word

Promotion is different from persuasion. Promotion is letting moms know about your group, and how they can find out more, so they can determine if they want to be involved. Persuasion is trying to convince moms why they should join your group. Persuasion is not a bad thing, unless it makes the focus of someone's decision what *you* want them to do instead of what *God* wants them do.

> God knows what He's doing to build your group, and that gives you freedom simply to be a good promoter who trusts the Holy Spirit to do the persuading.

God knows what He's doing to build your group, and that gives you freedom simply to be a good promoter who trusts the Holy Spirit to do the persuading. Even Paul, the greatest apostle, said of himself: "I was with you in weakness and in fear and in much trembling, and my message and my preaching were not in persuasive words of wisdom, but in demonstration of the Spirit and of power, so that your faith would not rest on the wisdom of men, but on the power of God" (1 Corinthians 2:3-5). Similarly, let someone decide to come to your group because of the "power of God," not just because of your "persuasive words of wisdom."

George Mueller, the nineteenth century British minister, is known for not asking donors for money for his ministry to orphans. Instead, he would pray and wait, trusting God to provide. The same principle can be true of your group. Don't get anxious about getting women to join. Rather, tell them what you're doing, and why, and then trust God to bring the moms who need to be there.

Below are some suggestions to help you get started on promoting your group to moms. You don't have to do them all!

- **Word of Mouth** – Begin telling people you know. These are likely existing friends you have through church, a group, your neighborhood, or your children's sports and community activities. Tell your friends to tell their friends! Create an attractive email to send out to your friends (insert a small photo of yourself to make it more personal). Share regularly about your developing group on Facebook, Twitter, and any other social media you use.

- **Printed Materials** – Create a simple half–page handout or full-page flyer about your group. If needed, ask a friend who enjoys graphic arts on the computer to design it for you. Promotional materials printed in color are more likely to be read. If you want to reach out, identify possible places to distribute your materials, such as in the church bulletin or on the visitor's table, a community center, a support group or co-op, or a Christian bookstore. You never know which location will be the one that reaches a ready mom.

- **Leaders and Gatekeepers** – Identify ministry and community leaders who are in touch with women who might benefit from your group, and let those leaders know what you're doing–your pastor, your church women's ministry leader, family and children's pastors, a homeschooling support group leader, leaders in other churches. You don't need to persuade them about your group; just let them know what you're doing and ask them to let others know.

- **Digital Connections –** To stay connected with your group members, plan to use digital resources and social media. Start by creating an email list to communicate with interested moms (be sure to have their permission to send them an email). Then create a Facebook group where you can post regular news and updates, and possibly a Twitter account to post short messages. If you are so inclined, you can create a free blog (such as Wordpress.com or Blogger.com) where you can describe your group and share your thoughts and insights. If there is a Facebook Mom Heart page for your city, be sure to announce your group there.

# HINTS: THE MEMBERS

## Owning Your Leadership

- » **Testimony:** Be prepared in your heart and mind to share your vision for your Mom Heart group with others outside your group who ask about it. It is not prideful for you to be positive, hopeful, and optimistic about your group.

- » **First Meeting:** When you meet for the first time, share your journey of starting and leading the group–how

God put it on your heart, why you felt you needed a group, how God opened doors, what you envision the group becoming. Your story will help the others in your group feel they are part of something God is doing.

» **Questions:** Being the leader of the group does not mean that you need to have an answer for every question. It simply means you will be willing to help find an answer, or see that someone else in the group does.

» **False Humility:** A new leader can feel uncomfortable as the "out front" person. They might feel the need to be quiet and constrained out of a misplaced fear of being perceived as prideful. However, don't let a false humility deprive the others in your group of the leadership they will be looking for. You can be confident in Christ.

» **Discussion Guide:** One of the challenging but necessary tasks of a group leader is getting back to and staying on topic if group discussion veers into critical comments or disagreements about churches or denominations, political issues, personal preferences (movies, music, and such), educational choices, parenting styles, or other conflicting opinions. Take the lead to end that discussion and get back on the topic.

# Notes

_____

_____

_____

_____

_____

_____

_____

_____

_____

_____

_____

_____

_____

_____

_____

_____

_____

_____

_____

_____

_____

# Section 3
# THE MEETING

**Members are the makings a group, but a group is actually made by meetings.** When you gather with other mothers with a common purpose, you are creating the "ties that bind." When you meet together physically as friends and fellow members of a body, you also meet spiritually. Christianity is not an aggregation of individuals; it is congregations of members of Christ's body. We cannot become "one in Christ" without meetings. Your Mom Heart group meeting is where your hearts as mothers will beat as one, and where you'll learn to live to the beat of God's heart for mothers.

Our children's hearts long to be a part of a great cause. Training our children for ministry is at the center of everything we are attempting to do in their lives. Serving God is not about knowing all the right rules and keeping them; it is about cultivating compassion in the hearts of our children for a lost world and showing them how they can practically be a part of His plans to reach the world.

~*The Mom Walk*, Sally Clarkson

# SERVING YOUR MOM HEART GROUP

T hroughout the Bible, we see examples of God's people gathering together to serve, love, encourage, pray, worship, and learn with one another. In the early chapters of the book of Acts, the church is described as gathering regularly for the purpose of engaging in very specific activities together, both in large gatherings and in small home gatherings. Those meetings were not random and unplanned, but purposeful and thoughtfully prepared (see: Acts 2:43-47).

Meetings are a fact of Christian life. Some will be characterized by "letting the Spirit lead," which can be appropriate for some gatherings. Sometimes it is best to just let God lead the meeting. Other meetings, though, will be characterized by someone "leading by the Spirit," which generally means the leader has an agenda and a plan for the time. When a meeting is directed by someone who has prayerfully and carefully thought about the purpose of the meeting, they can help to make that time more purposeful, efficient, and effective. It's not about controlling the meeting, but about directing it. And a leader who is "leading by the

Spirit" will do so in the spirit of Christ and with what is best for others in mind (see: Galatians 5:22-26; Philippians 2:1-4).

While your primary aim should be to create a meaningful meeting for all the moms who are involved in your group, it should be about more than only pursuing your purpose or accomplishing your plans. Your goal should be to create a meeting environment that is safe, comfortable, enjoyable, under control, and free of unnecessary distractions. That kind of meeting atmosphere will not happen by accident. It requires thoughtful planning, humility, and of course the leading of the Holy Spirit.

As the group leader, you are like the director of a symphony—you orchestrate many different elements to create refreshing and beautiful spiritual music that is melodic and harmonious. It may take some time to get everyone together on the same notes and on the same beat, but when it happens it will be delightful and powerful.

The following principles of group leadership are not rules or laws, but wisdom principles drawn from Scripture and life. Following them will help insure that your group makes beautiful music together.

## Be Prepared: Honor Your Group with Readiness

Serving any size of group well includes preparing well. We all know the awkwardness of being in a meeting when the leader is not prepared—it can be uncomfortable, unresponsive, and unproductive. We also know what it's like when a group leader is well-prepared—it inspires confidence that invites responsiveness and participation. Of course, we also know the discomfort of sitting under a controlling and overbearing leader, but that model has absolutely no place in a Mom Heart group. A Mom Heart group leader should be ready, prepared, confident, and gracious.

As a leader, your readiness for your group meeting will make you more relaxed and confident, and that will make your group members more relaxed, receptive, and responsive. Your preparedness doesn't mean that your group will automatically be responsive to you, but it does mean that you'll be more likely not to be caught off guard, and you can confidently navigate the

> The better prepared you are the better you will be able to encourage the kind of group interaction and discussion that will make your group a delight to all who are there.

inevitable potholes and speed bumps that happen in every group. Your readiness will help you know better how to lead and respond to the group.

There are few things more frustrating for a small group leader than a passive and unresponsive group. The better prepared you are the better you will be able to encourage the kind of group interaction and discussion that will make your group a delight to all who are there. Your preparedness actually gives the Holy Spirit more room to work in and through your moms' hearts. Here are a few helpful tips on being ready:

- **Pray for Your Group** – Spend time praying for the moms in your group throughout the week. They will sense your concern for their needs when you meet, and that will make them more receptive to your leadership and willing to participate in group discussions. Pray also for your own spirit of service, your ministry of leadership, the dynamics and relationships of the group, and for the details surrounding the group meeting. Pray for

God's grace to saturate all that you do. Prayer is spiritual preparation for leading your group with spiritual power.

- **Prepare for Your Lesson** – Start preparing your lesson well in advance. If you wait until the last minute, your authority as a leader will last about a minute. Give yourself plenty of time during the week to read the group materials or book, do the Bible study or discussion questions, and prepare your HEART lesson plan (see Section 5: The Model–Leading Your Mom Heart Group). The more time you give yourself to review and become familiar with the material, the more time you give God to get the lesson from your head into your heart. When it is only in your head, you can teach with personal authority; when it is also in your heart, you will lead and teach with spiritual authority and confidence.

- **Plan for Your Meeting** – The old adage is still true: If you fail to plan, you plan to fail. The devil is in the details of even the smallest small group, but just a little advance planning will help deter devilish distractions. Any small area of detail fail–handouts, refreshments, babysitter– can leave you frustrated and distracted when you need to be focused. Use the Mom Heart Group Planning Sheet (see: Section 10) to make sure the devilish details are covered–meeting area is organized, materials are printed and available, volunteer helpers know their responsibilities, refreshments are purchased and ready ahead of time, child care workers are scheduled, reminder emails about the meeting are sent, and whatever else needed is done. If you will be meeting somewhere other than in your own home, review the meeting plans with your host, and be sure to let her or the facility manager know that you will plan to arrive thirty minutes before the meeting begins (earlier if you are responsible for any setup).

## Be Hospitable: Serve Your Group with Enthusiasm

As a mother with time in the trenches, you have by now learned one important truth by experience: Motherhood is delightful, but it can also be demanding and daunting. The daily piling on of duties, responsibilities, crises, conflicts, and needs can leave even the most capable mom feeling tired, alone, discouraged, and overwhelmed. When moms come to your group meeting, the demands of motherhood can sometimes weigh heavily on them. Carrying that weight can drain the delights of motherhood from their spirits, and that can affect the spirit of your group.

> You have the power to create a space for moms in your group to feel loved, encouraged, and refreshed. How? Simply by creating a home characterized by hospitality.

When you see a mom with that weight walking in your door, her burden is not something you need to correct. After all, she is coming to the Mom Heart group to be with others who will share in that burden with her. It should not be corrected, but it can be deflected. You have the power to create a space for moms in your group to feel loved, encouraged, and refreshed. How? Simply by creating a home characterized by hospitality.

According to Dictionary.com, hospitality is "the quality or disposition of receiving and treating guests and strangers in a warm, friendly, generous way." The biblical terms suggest the idea of welcoming strangers and others into your fellowship. Hospitality is primarily expressed in the act of welcoming others into your home, but it is more; it is also the intention of creating a welcoming home. We like to suggest two qualities that create a hospitable home: atmosphere and environment.

The *atmosphere* of hospitality is the spiritual air that your guests will breathe in—the tones of joy, enthusiasm, and anticipation; the spirit of grace, gentleness, and love; the sense of God's life and truth; the priority on people and relationship. The *environment* of hospitality is the surroundings that your guests will experience—the orderliness and ambiance of a room that makes it inviting, comfortable, and attractive; thoughtful décor that adds life, beauty, color, and texture; inviting, tasteful refreshments that are creative, healthy, and presented nicely; selected music, art, and books that add fullness and meaning.

You may be thinking, "I understand about the atmosphere of hospitality, and can do that. But I don't know about the environment part. We don't have nice things, and I'm not a good decorator." But consider this: If atmosphere is the verbal expression of welcome, then environment is the nonverbal. A welcoming home environment says loudly and clearly to your guests that they are important enough to you that you have thoughtfully prepared a place of welcome for them. It does not take much to create a welcoming and hospitable environment that will "speak" to your guest. And when you do, it will also strengthen and enhance the personal atmosphere you create. This is true even if you are meeting in a neutral, non-home facility—whatever you do to improve the environment will also improve the atmosphere. It just takes a little extra time and effort. Perhaps that's why Paul exhorts Christians, "Practice hospitality" (Romans 12:13 NIV). Following are a few hospitali-tips.

- **Greeter:** Plan to have a greeter ready to open the door and welcome the moms into your home. Give your greeter some simple guidelines for the welcome—smile and make eye contact, greet warmly with their name, offer a touch or hug, show interest and ask questions, direct them where to go, connect them with another mom.

- **Name Badges:** If your group is larger, or often has moms who don't always know one another, don't neglect to have some simple name badges on hand. Part of hospitality is removing the awkwardness of not knowing names, or not being known. It is just a simple courtesy for those who are new to the group.

- **Meeter:** As the group leader, make it your goal to meet and interact with each woman as they enter your home and before the meeting time. Depending on the size of the group, it may be just a brief encounter, but a touch, eye contact, and their name will go a long way to making them feel noticed and welcomed.

- **Refreshments:** Even if you plan to have refreshments after your meeting, offer your group members coffee, tea, or a beverage when they arrive. It lets them know you have prepared for them, and it provides an easy way to create connections and stimulate conversation before the meeting time. Consider it hospitality fuel.

- **Seating:** When the room you will meet in has been prepared for the meeting, with comfortable seating thoughtfully arranged, it tells the group members that you have thought about them. Seating should never be an afterthought, hastily pulled together just before the meeting.

- **Candles:** Even in a sunlit room, lighted candles can add a physical and spiritual warmth to a home, reminding of Christ's light and life. Keep extra candles of all sizes on hand. Votive or tea candles in glass holders are simple ways to add some candle light.

- **Music:** Music is like emotional light. The right selection of background music can create a specific emotional tone to your home—inspirational, celebrational, reflective, casual, fun, or whatever you feel is appropriate. You can turn it off for the meeting time, but having it on when moms arrive can help shape the atmosphere of your home.

## Be Protective: Cover Your Group with Security

Have you ever had a confidence broken? A secret revealed by a friend? A fear or failure shared privately exposed publicly? A past deed you have tried to forget revived? Your reputation stained by malicious gossip? Your behavior or values demeaned by a critic? If you have, then you know what it feels like to have your private life violated.

> One of your highest priorities as a Mom Heart group leader is to assure every mom that she is in a safe and secure group.

The embarrassment, anger, or fear passes, but the inevitable end result is distrust, withdrawal, and self-protection. When safety leaves, so does the person. When a group is not safe, it will not thrive, and may not survive.

One of your highest priorities as a Mom Heart group leader is to assure every mom that she is in a safe and secure group. She needs to have confidence that anything she shares with the group, other than illegal or harmful behavior, will be held in strict confidence by the others. Foster an environment where everyone feels comfortable, respected, and honored. As a leader, you will create the tone that will make your members feel that it is safe for them to share and learn together.

We reject legalism in any form. However, we do uphold three guiding "laws" that we expect each Mom Heart group to accept and enforce. These are not unbiblical laws of belief or behavior that will separate and judge; rather, they are biblical laws of relationship that will protect and guide. The purpose of each "shalt not" below is to help you cultivate and maintain the safety and security of your group.

- **Thou Shalt Not Betray** – Betrayal of any kind–of a trust, confidence, secret, fear, or past sin–creates an atmosphere of distrust in a group. Establish a clear standard of group loyalty and confidentiality early, remind members of it regularly, and intervene immediately if you hear anything that could threaten it. It is up to you to protect the covenant of mutual trust that grows out of sharing personal needs and struggles. Betrayal wounds hearts, and will severely, if not irreparably, damage your group. You are protecting not only the moms' hearts in your group, but also the integrity of your Mom Heart group.

- **Thou Shalt Not Gossip** – Scripture declares that gossip is a serious sin. Paul includes gossip in his lists of sins that include wickedness, greed, murder, envy, slander, and many more (Romans 1:28-32; 2 Corinthians 12:20). In Titus 2:3-5 he says, "Older women likewise are to be reverent in their behavior, not malicious gossips." Gossip most often occurs in the form of unguarded conversation about people and affairs outside of the group. Enforce a no-gossip policy (and beware the gossip-driven prayer request!). Gossip is a destructive poison that can infect the spirit of your group and kill it. Constrain gossip, and be ready to confront it if necessary.

- **Thou Shalt Not Judge** – A judgmental attitude in some large ministries can be grounds for dismissal. A staff member with a consistently critical spirit is a negative and corrosive influence on others, and especially on group unity and cohesiveness. The same is true for a Mom Heart small group or ministry. You've probably encountered someone with a judgmental attitude or spirit–new ideas are negated or neutralized, weaknesses and flaws are pointed out in leaders, motives and attitudes are judged, events and activities are criticized, and on it goes. As the group leader, be alert to a judgmental or critical spirit, and don't hesitate to lovingly confront it if necessary.

## Be Encouraging: Influence Your Group with Godliness

The Apostle Paul encouraged believers with the truth that had been revealed to him by God, but he also encouraged them with his own example of how that truth is lived out through a godly life (see: 2 Corinthians 4:1-15; 1 Thessalonians 2:10-12). Paul preached and practiced what he believed. Several times in Scripture, Paul holds up his own life to others as an example to follow and emulate. As a follower of Christ and a leader, your goal should be no different–that your life would be an example to others. As the leader of your group, you have the opportunity to encourage your moms to believe God and to be faithful.

The biblical idea of encouragement is typically represented by the Greek verb *parakaleo*. It is a compound of two Greek words—*para*, alongside; and *kaleo*, to call. Literally it means to "call alongside," but can be translated as encourage, exhort, or comfort. The encourager is one who comes alongside another to help as they walk with Christ. Being that kind of encourager is a key part of your role as a Mom Heart group leader—to come alongside each mom in your group and encourage them in their life with Christ. One of the greatest gifts you will give to your group is godly, biblical encouragement.

You may not feel qualified or gifted enough to think that you could be a godly encourager like Paul, but remember that you have the same Holy Spirit that Paul did. If God calls you to a ministry, He will equip and empower you by His Spirit to do it (see: Philippians 4:12-13; 2 Peter 1:2-11). You can expect spiritual battles tempting you to feel discouraged, inadequate, or afraid, but the

> As a group leader, you "infuse your group with grace" when your discussions and teaching bring spiritual delight to your moms—spirits are lifted, burdens are eased, and faith is affirmed.

Spirit of God will come alongside you to encourage you, to help you find courage through Christ. Paul's pastoral protégé, Timothy, apparently was timid and lacked courage. In his very last letter, Paul encouraged Timothy with these words: "God did not give you a spirit of timidity, but a spirit of power, of love, and of self-discipline" (2 Timothy 1:7). The same Spirit is at work in your life. Being a godly encourager is not about what you can do, but what the Spirit can do through you.

## Be Loving: Infuse Your Group with Grace

The New Testament is full of grace. We pray that every Mom Heart group also will be full of grace. The Greek word *charis*, which means a "gracious benefit bestowed," appears about a hundred times in the New Testament. You probably know the many familiar passages about God's grace *toward* us in salvation (Ephesians 2:8-10), but God's grace is also expressed *through* us in our relationships with one another.

We all know the definition of grace as the "unmerited favor" of God, but its most basic meaning is "that which causes delight." Grace is the delightful goodness of God made available to us in Christ, but it is also that goodness expressed through us to others. In other words, grace characterizes a lifestyle that offers others the same favor and delight we have found in God, in contrast to the burden that rules and laws place on the spirit.

As a group leader, you "infuse your group with grace" when your discussions and teaching bring spiritual delight to your moms—spirits are lifted, burdens are eased, and faith is affirmed. Rather than guilt, condemnation, or shame, moms will find the grace that Jesus offers through His Spirit—love, hope, mercy, forgiveness, freedom, help, encouragement, edification, gentleness, patience, longsuffering, and joy in the Lord. They see Jesus in the grace they see in you and receive from you.

In his letter to the Galatians, Paul made clear that those who taught a Christianity of keeping laws and rules were living by the flesh (sin), not by the Spirit. "It was for freedom that Christ set us free [from slavery to law]" (5:1), and that freedom is found only in living by the Spirit—by the law of love that God has written on our hearts, not by the old Law of external rules and regulations. Grace sets us free to set others free to live in the Spirit by the law of love that Christ taught (John 15:12-17). Grace brings freedom.

Most Christians rightly teach that we are no longer to live by the demands of the Jewish Law, but too many then turn around and preach that we need to live by Christian laws— rules that will, they claim, make us acceptable to God. They will try to convince others that "real" Christians need to believe or behave according to their way in order to be acceptable to God, and to them. Rather than creating true unity in the Spirit, their "Christian law" only creates barriers to fellowship through disunity, guilt, and condemnation. But that is not the teaching of Christ or the apostles. And it should never be the teaching of a Mom Heart group.

Infusing your group with grace does not mean that sin is glossed over or overlooked. John said, "For the Law was given through Moses; grace and truth were realized through Jesus Christ" (John 1:17). Truth is always just as much a part of being Christ to others as is grace, and they are found in perfect balance in Christ. As those called to be like Christ, we are to offer truth balanced with grace. If you study God's truth in your group in an atmosphere of grace, you will bring delight to your moms' hearts.

# HINTS: The Meeting

## Getting Together Purposefully

» **Assistance:** Ask your ministry partner to come thirty minutes before your group starts to help with last-minute preparations, and to pray together.

Encouragement and a peaceful spirit will help you lead your group confidently.

» **Safety:** Don't try to force openness and honesty from a group member. Prying or cajoling a reluctant mom to open up, even if done good naturedly, can feel to her like an invasion of her private life, and make the group feel unsafe to her.

» **Connection:** Times have changed, and now the best way to stay in touch with a group of women is through an online connection such as Facebook. Start a Facebook group and invite women to join. You can create community, make announcements, keep a calendar, share prayer requests, post good links, and more. If you choose to make your Facebook group open, other women who may not be able to attend your Mom Heart group can still benefit from the community.

» **First Meeting:** Spend your first meeting just getting to know one another. Create an inviting atmosphere and provide a delicious dessert and beverages. Ask each mom ahead of time to prepare a two or three minute talk about their history, family, and hopes. We call it a "mintro" (minute intro). Be ready with some creative discussion questions: What are five adjectives that describe you? What are the most and least enjoyable things about your life? If you had unlimited funds, where would you want to live and raise your children? What is a "hidden talent" that most people don't know about you?

# Notes

# Section 4

# THE MINISTRY

**If anyone should be ministered to in the body of Christ, it should be mothers.** They labor to bring new life into the world, provide life-giving nourishment and protection for their innocent infant, and sacrifice their own life and plans for the benefit of a growing child which has no plans other than to be a child. And yet, even so, it is mothers who often do the serving of others. A Mom Heart group is one place where the ministry focus is on the mother. After all, who better knows their needs than another mother? When hearts meet, ministry happens.

As a mother...I, too, have a need to "walk in the Light as He Himself is in the Light," as John reminded Jesus' followers (1 John 1:7). I need to give my thought processes to the Lord—to reject fear and focus on the reality of the Lord's love and power. As I model such disciplined thinking for my children and as I train them how to think for themselves, I not only arm them for their future spiritual battles; I also arm myself.

~*The Ministry of Motherhood,* Sally Clarkson

# Nurturing Your Mom Heart Group

One of the words for nurture in the New Testament is the Greek term *ektrepho*, which literally means "to feed from." Paul said husbands were to *ektrepho* their wives (Ephesians 5:29, "nourish"), and fathers their children (6:4, "bring them up"). Biblical nurture is the act of feeding another person from the life of God that is already in your own life. That is one of the privileges you have as a Mom Heart group leader—to nurture the life of Christ in other moms out of your own life with Him. You can facilitate a group atmosphere that will encourage that kind of nurture. Creating that kind of life-giving dynamic in your group will come mostly from your own personal ministry of nurture with each individual woman.

A Mom Heart group provides a unique way to have a personal ministry. Perhaps you think that sounds like something you don't feel equipped to do—to personally engage another mom and minister to her. But nurturing someone else is not difficult or scary, requires no special training, and can make a difference in that person's life. We believe that God has enabled every believer, not just the professional clergy, to have a personal ministry. As a group leader, you exercise a personal ministry of influence and encouragement in a mom's life simply by spiritually nurturing her.

Many moms will never be nurtured spiritually. Don't let that be the experience of the moms God brings to your group. The personal ministry of spiritual nurture should be as natural and nonthreatening as meeting for coffee. It's not about following a formula, but simply about purposeful and meaningful fellowship in Christ. To help you create nurturing moments with your moms, we've created an acrostic out of MOM to suggest three things you can do.

## M – Meet Purposefully with Each Mother

Make it a goal to meet with each mom in your Mom Heart group at least one time during a season of study, more if possible.

> Following the pattern in Paul's words—affirmation, confirmation, expectation—suggests a simple, three-part model for how to make every meeting with your moms a time of purposeful fellowship.

Purpose in your heart ahead of time to make your meeting a meaningful time of biblical fellowship, or *koinonia*. In the New Testament, that word signifies a "communion of intimate participation" between followers of Jesus (see: Acts 2:42-47). Paul thanks God and prays for the Philippian church that brings him joy because of their "participation [*koinonia*] in the gospel" with him. He affirms his affection for them, confirms his confidence in God's work in their lives, and shares his expectation of their continued growth and obedience (see: Philippians 1:3-11). Following the pattern in Paul's words—affirmation, confirmation, expectation—suggests a simple, three-part model for how to make every meeting with your moms a time of purposeful fellowship.

We all love getting together socially with a special friend for no other reason than just to relax. We all need a respite now and then for refreshment and enjoyment. However, if you want a time together to be about true biblical fellowship, you will need to be intentional and purposeful about it. It may start out as a casual time of getting to know one another, or even as a serious time to guide and counsel on topics or issues too sensitive for the larger group setting. However, regardless of whatever reason brings you together, you can always turn any meeting into a time of spiritual nurturing.

> In an increasingly fragmented and impersonal world, the art of initiating purposefully into another person's life is being lost in the flood of digital, social, and spiritual substitutes.

Only one thing will prevent this kind of nurturing ministry from happening—failure to initiate. If you don't initiate, then you won't participate. Implicit in the concept of *koinonia* fellowship is reaching out to those with whom you share the life of God. In an increasingly fragmented and impersonal world, the art of initiating purposefully into another person's life is being lost in the flood of digital, social, and spiritual substitutes. As a Mom Heart leader, you can have a true spiritual impact on the moms in your group, but only if you choose to initiate and meet with them. Here are some tips for meeting:

- Initiate and work out a time with the mom that will be convenient for both of you. Get each mom on your calendar early in the season of your group. Be sure to ask about child care.

- Select a familiar meeting place such as your home, a

favorite coffee spot, or a park. Wherever you choose, be sure it allows for private, intimate, and uninterrupted conversation.

- Have a personal ACE message (**A**ffirmation, **C**onfirmation, **E**xpectation) ready in your mind, or even on a note in your Bible. Just taking some time to thoughtfully prepare those statements will create a sense of purpose and meaning in your mind for the meeting.

- Call or send a personal email reminder the day before your meeting expressing how much you look forward to the time. Share a meaningful Scripture or quote.

- Offer to pick up the mom and drive to the meeting location. The drive can provide time for small talk so you can move on to more important conversation when you meet.

## O – Offer Thoughtfully Biblical Encouragement

When Jewish Christians in the early church were forced to leave Jerusalem because of the persecution, they were scattered to distant locations where they no longer had familiar people and places to count on for spiritual security. They were far from home and on their own. So listen to what the writer of Hebrews told them: "And let us consider how we may spur one another on toward love and good deeds. Let us not give up meeting together, as some are in the habit of doing, but let us encourage one another—and all the more as you see the Day approaching" (Hebrews 10:24-25, NIV). We, too, are far from home and on our own. Your role as a Mom

Heart leader is to offer the love and encouragement that your moms need as they are looking for spiritual security in their journey through life as a mother. You can do that best by encouraging them from God's Word.

The writer of Hebrews also said that "the word of God is living and active" (4:12). Paul, in his last written words, said that every bit of Scripture is "God-breathed and is useful for teaching, rebuking, correcting and training in righteousness, so that the man [or mom] of God may be thoroughly equipped for every good work" (2 Timothy 3:16-17 NIV). The psalmist affirmed to God, "Your word is a lamp to my feet and a light to my path" (Psalm 119:102). Jesus ended His sermon on the mount with the reminder that "everyone who hears these words of mine and acts on them" will be like the wise man who "built his house on the rock" rather than on shifting sand (Matthew 7:24-27). Here's the basic truth: The Bible, God's Word, is living and active, working within us to guide us, help us mature, equip us for kingdom work, and enable us to weather the storms of life.

> When you meet with each of your moms, plan to make God's Word part of your conversation.

When you meet with each of your moms, plan to make God's Word part of your conversation. There may be a "by the Spirit" Bible verse that will come up as you talk, but you should also be prepared ahead of time "by the Spirit" with thoughtful verses you've selected. That just means you plan ahead to bring the spiritual nurture and nourishment that you know will encourage your moms. And don't be afraid to paraphrase a passage if you need to—you're just sharing the heart of what God has spoken to you. Here are a few practical ways you can feed and encourage with God's Word when you meet:

- Pray about what encouragement you think each mom might need and have some selected Scriptures in mind when you meet. Write them down, or mark the pages in your Bible.

- Ask thoughtful questions and listen carefully before you offer Scripture for encouragement or advice. Share your insights the same way you'd like someone to share Scripture with you.

- Wait for a natural time to share a Scripture. Be careful not to emotionally ambush your friend with God's Word, or force it unnaturally into a narrow opening.

- Rather than applying a Scripture to your friend, talk about how it has helped you personally. Sharing truth as personal testimony can be just as effective as offering a specific biblical admonition.

- If you have personal counsel or advice to offer, anchor it in biblical truth or wisdom.

- After your meeting, send a note of encouragement to that mom with selected scriptures that you discussed.

## M – Make Meaningful Prayer a Priority

"Rejoice always; pray without ceasing; in everything give thanks; for this is God's will for you in Christ Jesus" (1 Thessalonians 5:16-18). Paul was not saying that prayer is the *only* thing you should do; rather, he was saying that prayer should be a part of *everything* you do. Worship, intercession, thanksgiving, submission—these all are aspects of a healthy prayer life. Prayer is an ongoing conversation with God. When you meet with a mom and encourage her from God's Word, the natural and normal response to hearing from God should be to talk to God.

Remember that you are offering spiritual nurture to the mom you are meeting with, feeding her from the life of Christ in your own heart. In case you missed it, this MOM acrostic has spelled out three channels of what could be called "means of grace." You are nurturing a mom by opening windows of God's grace into her heart through fellowship (God

> When you pray, you are acknowledging by faith that "he who comes to God must believe that He is and that He is a rewarder of those who seek Him"

speaking to and through you), God's Word (God speaking to you), and prayer (you speaking to God). When those windows are opened, God's grace—the gift of his favor and blessing—can flow into an open heart. By doing those three very simple things, you are bringing life-giving grace into that mom's mind and heart.

All three of the above ways to nurture are important, but prayer is the key to this triad of nurturing grace—it is what turns your focus and attention from yourself onto the living God. When you pray, you are acknowledging by faith that "he who comes to God must believe that He is and that He is a rewarder of those who seek Him" (Hebrews 11:6). Here are some suggestions for how to make prayer a natural and meaningful part of your MOM time:

- Don't force prayer into your time together, but be sensitive to appropriate times to stop and pray about an issue, or to close your time together with a short prayer. If a natural time to pray doesn't happen, simply ask, "How can I be praying for you," and assure her you'll pray later.

- Be aware of your environment. If you're in a small coffee

shop with others in close proximity, pray when you get to your car. Even mature believers can feel self-conscious praying in public where others can watch and listen.

- Be aware of the mom for whom you are praying. If you sense or discern that there is any discomfort with praying in public, then don't. She is the priority, not the need to make prayer happen. Ask how you can pray for her later.

- Be discerning about what kind of prayer will be appropriate, whether it should be short or can be longer, and how personal you should be in your prayer. If a matter seems sensitive, just ask, "Do you mind if I pray about that?"

- If you aren't able to pray together in person, call the mom and pray on the phone with her. If you're both comfortable with tech and connectivity, you can pray together on a video call by Skype or FaceTime.

- Pray regularly for each of the moms in your group in your own personal prayer times. Send them a text or email to let them know that you've prayed for them.

- Keep a written or digital record of special prayer requests by each mom, or specific needs for which you have prayed. Ask each mom privately how God has responded. This record of prayers should be private, secured, and not shared publicly. Unless you have her permission, it should remain only between you and the other mom.

# HINTS: The Ministry

## Making Spiritual Friendships

» **Gifts:** A thoughtful gift can be a powerful way to express love and friendship. It can be as simple as some flowers, or something very personalized or meaningful. A special teacup can create a bond; a framed calligraphy Bible verse can encourage in a hard time; a figurine can express symbolic meaning or commemorate an event. Be creative with your gifts.

» **Books:** A book specifically chosen and given at the right time can be both a meaningful and a helpful gift. Inscribe it with a personal note and a relevant scripture.

» **Photos:** Photographs are visually captured memories. A fun or memorable photo turned into a print and specially framed can become a treasured gift. Use a no-bleed fine point Sharpie to record the place and date on the back.

» **Music:** Music is personal. When you learn a mom's musical liked and you give her a music CD that reflects her personal musical tastes, it is a way of affirming who she is, and appreciating what she likes.

» **Potlucks:** "Go into all the world and have potlucks." There was always a bit of truth in that humorous commentary on small church mission. Meals are important in Scripture, and important in our lives. Eating together is a biblically-affirmed fellowship experience. Thank God it is! Plan potlucks, picnics, repasts, progressive dinners, and other food-centered events into your group calendar. "Eat, drink, and be merry!"

» **Holidays:** Reserve a spot on your group calendar early in the season for holiday get-togethers. Holiday events are great times to get the husbands involved. Have a dessert night and carol-sing at Christmas; plan a Valentine Day potluck with a rom-com movie; have a spring fling in the park with a picnic and family fun day.

# Notes

# Section 5
# THE MODEL

**Christianity was birthed out of Judaism.** The meetings and ministry of the earliest Jewish Christians were not something new, but modeled after what they had always done as Jews. The home and the synagogue were models for the new community of believers. The HEART model you will learn for leading a Mom Heart group lesson is not something new; it uses priorities drawn from familiar and well-seasoned models for teaching and talking about God's Word. We don't reinvent the wheel; we just make it a bit more attractive and usable.

I know that I must prepare [my children's] minds with biblical truth and a Christian worldview if they are to keep the faith in a hostile world. What they become as adults and what they do with their lives will depend in large measure on what they know about God. If I want their lights to shine brightly in the darkness that pervades this world, then I must light strong fires of truth in their minds now.

*~Seasons of a Mother's Heart,* Sally Clarkson

# LEADING YOUR MOM HEART GROUP

You probably have heard it taught that the church is both a living *organism* and a functional *organization*—the dynamic and gifted body of Christ led by the Holy Spirit, as well as the orderly and structured gathering of God's people led by its leaders. Both qualities are important, and both are necessary.

In the early chapters of the book of Acts, the church is alive with the Holy Spirit, growing organically with new believers, and rapidly increasing wherever the Spirit touches lives. However, as the church grows it also is being organized to support and direct all the new souls being added to its numbers. In Acts 2:42, the dynamic new church is already settling into a purposeful structure of "devoting themselves to the apostles' teaching and to fellowship, to the breaking of bread and to prayer." They are meeting both in large groups in the temple courts for teaching, and in small groups in houses for fellowship and worship (Acts 2:43-47).

Mom Heart groups are modeled after the small groups seen in the early church in Acts—Christians gathering to share their lives and to hear from and respond to God. Mom Heart groups meet to encourage, equip, and enable moms to start, lead, and tend small groups of mothers. That is our mission. As part of the equipping aspect of our mission, we have created an uncomplicated, effective teaching model that you can use for leading your small group meeting time. It is designed both to cultivate the organic nature of your group meeting, and to regulate its organizational structure. The HEART small group lesson model provides both flexibility and orderliness in a simple and memorable meeting template.

> Mom Heart groups are modeled after the small groups seen in the early church in Acts—Christians gathering to share their lives and to hear from and respond to God.

There are, of course, countless ways to lead a small group, and many teachers have their own favorite lesson outlines to follow. The most popular teaching models tend to share similar priorities, but simply express them in different creative ways. For example, for many years a common small group Bible study and discussion model has been the "Hook, Book, Look, Took" approach popularized by Dr. Larry Richards—gain attention, talk about the passage, apply it personally, express it in life. That pattern has been imitated by many other teachers.

For Mom Heart groups, we have created our own model using the acrostic HEART. It follows roughly the same pattern as other models, except that it uses the priorities of inductive Bible study as guides for study—invitation, observation, interpretation, application, and supplication. You may not be familiar with the terms deductive and inductive Bible study, Deductive Bible study starts with a topic and studies Scripture to explain it, like a detective gathering clues to solve a case. Inductive Bible study starts with a passage and studies the

Scripture to learn what it has to say, like a historian studying source material to explain an event.

The HEART outline is modeled after an inductive study—we want each Mom Heart group to start with the Word to discover what God has to say through it to them. It is a model that begins with "Hear the Spirit" because it is about listening for God's voice, and ends with "Take It to Heart" because the purpose of Scripture is to change the life of the hearer. The goal of the HEART model is to insure that your group does not miss the "heart" of their time studying the Word together.

We believe that the HEART Bible study model is a unique teaching design that can help you create a rich and meaningful small group experience. You're free to use other models in creating your own lesson plan, but we encourage all of our Mom Heart group leaders to use the HEART model. Below are the five priorities of a HEART-shaped Mom Heart group meeting. The remainder of this chapter explains in detail how to use the model.

- **H** – Hear the Spirit (Invitation)
- **E** – Engage the Word (Observation)
- **A** – Affirm the Truth (Interpretation)
- **R** – Respond to God (Application)
- **T** – Take It to Heart (Supplication)

# H – Hear the Spirit

**Purpose:** To introduce the topic of the day's lesson with a nonthreatening discussion that generates interest, involvement, and interaction among group members, and sets the spirit for the lesson.

**Activity:** Invitation – What is the Bible talking about?

**Time:** 10-15 minutes

**Planning:** Invitation gets everyone on the same page. Create several discussion questions that will introduce the topic. Run them by family and friends to see if they are clear and understandable.

**Leading:**

The "Hear the Spirit" introduction is essentially a brief time of purposefully directed discussion. It sets the tone of the meeting, raises interest level in the topic, and allows everyone time to "warm up" to interacting as a group on deeper issues. You are not trying to elicit answers to questions, but to stimulate fun, meaningful, personal, or interesting discussion that is relevant to the topic. The goal is not to inform, but to engage everyone's participation in the discussion.

You may be tempted to think that this initial part of the HEART outline is not part of a "real" Bible study. You might convince yourself to pass over it quickly, or even just skip it, because "we have so much to cover today." Resist that thinking. In the same way that Jesus often took time to do some talking before telling, such as with the woman at the well (John 4:7-30), this time can be critical to setting the spirit of the rest of the meeting. The invitation is not just an "ice breaker" but a strategic part of the lesson that will help to connect and unify your group emotionally and spiritually. If you take this first step seriously, it will help your moms begin interacting personally and get them all headed in the same direction for the Bible study part of the lesson.

## Tips for Guiding "Hear the Spirit"

- Ask a general question about a common topic of interest, not a specific question about a biblical text you'll be studying and discussing. The former is open and inviting (everyone can have an opinion); the latter can be perceived as closed and threatening (no one wants to risk having the wrong answer).

- Create a discussion question that relates generally to the study, but that is broad enough that everyone can comment on it with an opinion or insight. Often, a lighter or even humorous question will generate easy discussion. It also helps to set up the question with some relevant personal comments or a story that will stimulate interest.

- As an example, if you were discussing John 1:1 ("In the beginning was the Word, and the Word was with God, and the Word was God"), you might ask your group: "What would your biographer write for an opening sentence in the book about your life?" or "What are three words that describe who you really are?" or "What 'in the beginning' word or term best describes each of your children?" or "What would it be like to be so close to someone that you are like one person?"

- In lieu of a general question, you can also read and discuss an interesting quote from someone historical or current, from a literary figure or author, from current news or commentary, or from a popular blog. You can also be really creative in this part of your meeting time: hold up an intriguing picture or a photograph, show a movie clip or an online video, play part of a song, or read an interesting poem and discuss it. Anything is an option if it leads you into the topic for the lesson.

# E – Engage the Word

**Purpose:** To read and discuss the Bible Study material for the day's lesson with the goal of identifying what God's Word has to say about the topic of study.

**Activity:** Observation – What does the Bible say?

**Time:** 30-45 minutes

**Planning:** Observation is the "head" of an inductive Bible study. You should invest extra time observing all that is in the passages being studied, using other study resources to see beneath the surface text.

**Leading:**

The "Engage the Word" part of your lesson is the focus of a Mom Heart group study. If you are doing a book study using one of Sally's books, or another author's, you can spend some time talking about the content of the chapter you read for the week. You also should have identified several specific Scripture passages from the chapter that can then become the Bible study portion of your time. Be sure to use the Mom Heart Group Lesson Planner form (see: Section 10) to write some good questions both for the book and for the identified scriptures. Your primary goal in this time is on reading and understanding what those scriptures are saying in relation to the author's message or topic.

You will need to guide the discussion to keep it centered primarily on observation—simply understanding what the Bible is saying about your topic. It is natural for the group to jump into interpretation and application, but try to gently guide the discussion back into more general observation at this point. Help your group put themselves in the original readers' time and circumstances in order hear the words in the same way those original recipients would have heard them. Dig out as many of the grammatical, linguistic, and historical gems from the passages as you can before moving on to interpretation.

## Tips for Guiding "Engage the Word"

- If you are using a book or other resource that already provides directed discussion questions for the chapter or lesson, be sure you have done them yourself the week before, and reviewed the questions prior to your group meeting. Write down your own personal observations about the Bible passages being studied, and then begin to create some group questions based on your own insights.

- Leading an effective Mom Heart group requires more than just reading questions and then waiting impatiently for answers, or worse, providing the answers yourself. You are not there to emcee a two-way Q&A time (you ask; they answer), but rather to stimulate a lively conversation among the group members. You are a facilitator, which means you are there to listen, draw out, engage, acknowledge, encourage, affirm, and direct. That's the real challenge and joy of being the leader of a Bible study or discussion group—leading others into a rich and meaningful conversation about God and His truth.

- You do not need to be a Bible scholar to lead a Mom Heart group discussion. However, the more you take time to study and review the passages of a lesson prior to your group, the easier and more effective it will be for you to lead a satisfying discussion. Build a small library of proven Bible study tools that will help you gain more insight into the passages of the lesson—a concordance for the Bible version you use; a Bible handbook or encyclopedia; a word study resource; a study Bible; and a topical Bible. You can also take advantage of free online Bible study websites, or Bible study software for your computer.

# A – Affirm the Truth

**Purpose:** To engage the group to synthesize one "big idea" that will express the content and the intent of the passages and material that have been studied and discussed in that day's lesson.

**Activity:** Interpretation – What does the Bible mean?

**Time:** 10-15 minutes

**Planning:** Interpretation is the "heart" of an inductive Bible study. Do your own interpretation first, then consult concordances, commentaries, and other helps to have a firm grasp on the material.

**Leading:**

The "Affirm the Truth" part of your meeting time is the next step of inductive Bible study—interpretation. In this step, you are helping your group extract the true meaning (God's intent) from the scriptures they have observed and discussed. It is part of the process that will move biblical truth from the head (intellectual) into the heart (personal). Interpretation is determining just what a passage means—what does God want you to know, to be, to do, or to believe about His truth. As you begin to answer any or all of those questions, you will be interpreting the author's content and intent.

Observation is mostly about information, but interpretation is about revelation. Interpretation is the step that makes us responsible for a response to what God has revealed. It is where we define what God's intent is in what He has said. At this point, you want your group to think about all the passages they have discussed and to summarize in one sentence the gist of God's heart or intent. One way to do that is to write a "Big Idea" sentence together. There are instructions on the next page for how to do that, or you can just come up with your own approach. The main thing is to summarize what you have discussed in one clear and concise statement.

## Tips for Guiding "Affirm the Truth"

- Be sure you take time prior to your group meeting to synthesize what you studied in the lesson into a summary statement of your own. It is not so you can tell the group what *you* think the study is all about, but so you can lead them to create *their own* "big idea" statement. Your knowledge of the lesson will enable you to direct them as they summarize the most important truths from the passages discussed into a statement.

- Don't linger too long on minutiae, but help the group quickly identify the most salient truths learned in that day's lesson and craft them into a single "big idea" sentence. It will help to have one of the members writing as the other members talk so you can be free to lead the discussion. The final sentence should be clear and concise so that it is a memorable "take home" thought that cogently summarizes what was learned that day.

- If you need a model for how to write a formal "Big Idea" statement, it's not hard to learn. It is simply a complete sentence with a subject and a complement. The subject expresses "What did the lesson talk about?" and the complement expresses "What did the lesson say about what was talked about?" The subject is not a single word such as discipleship, but rather the opening clause of a sentence: "Discipleship is an intentional relationship..." The complement completes the subject's thought. "Discipleship is an intentional relationship that requires training, instruction, and modeling."

- There is no right or wrong way for this summarization

exercise, so your group can be as flexible and creative as they want to be in crafting a "big idea" statement. If they seem hung up on the formal "Big Idea" form, just encourage them to put that aside and to write their own one sentence summary statement however they want to express it. The process is far more important than the product.

# R – Respond to God

**Purpose:** To encourage each mom in the group to take the time to write down a brief personal response or application to the lesson as expressed in the "big idea" statement.

**Activity:** Application – What does the Bible mean to me?

**Time:** 5 minutes

**Planning:** Application is the "hands" of an inductive Bible study. It is considering how God wants you, personally, to live out in your daily life and family the truths you have found in the passage.

**Leading:**

The "Respond to God" part of your meeting time is designed to provide a moment of quiet reflection in response to the Bible study and discussion. It is the third and final step of inductive Bible study–application. Encourage the group to consider quietly how the lesson, as expressed in the "big idea" that the group has just crafted together, impacts each of their lives personally. Remind them that there is no one way to respond, but that the Spirit of God can speak individually to each of them through the passages.

Encourage each mom to write down her personal application in the study guide or on a sheet of paper. This step is important because it allows the group members time to individually synthesize the head, heart, and hands truths that they have been discussing. Writing down thoughts can help to personalize and internalize lessons and truths learned from Bible study. This application step also prepares each group member to open her heart to God in prayer in the final part of the meeting. As the group leader, you should encourage the group to take this step seriously, and then be sure to model it as well in your own response to the lesson.

## Tips for Guiding "Respond to God"

- Use this step to bring the Bible study and discussion part of your group meeting to a natural ending point, and to create a brief but natural transition to the final part of the meeting time.

- Encourage everyone in the group to silently contemplate and reflect on the lesson you have just studied. Repeat the "big idea" summary statement just created. Give them just a few minutes (3-4) to write down their thoughts about what the Spirit of God might be saying to them personally. There's no form or format to the personal response. Explain that what they are writing is like a short personal journal entry.

- Some moms may not be accustomed to this kind of reflective response to Scripture, or may even be a bit resistant to going beyond just agreeing with the statement. You can "prime the pump" for everyone in the group by offering a bit of your own testimony as to what the Spirit says to you about the lesson. Keep it brief, succinct, and personal (i.e., don't start teaching or preaching about it). You're providing a model and example of how to hear God's Word and respond personally to it.

- Because this is a critical step in the HEART process, be sure you have pens and paper available so everyone can write down what they are thinking. Some may want to simply think about it, but encourage everyone to commit their thoughts to paper. There is a head and heart connection that happens in brain chemistry when mental words are written out. Writing can help to internalize a lesson.

# T – Take It to Heart

**Purpose:** To share and discuss personal responses to the lesson, and to pray together as a group about living out the truths learned in this lesson, and about needs of the group members.

**Activity:** Supplication – What does the Bible mean to us?

**Time:** 10-15 minutes

**Planning:** Supplication is the conclusion of your group study. Prepare beforehand a list of suggested prayers related to the study that you can offer during this time for prayer responses and requests.

## Leading:

The "Take It to Heart" conclusion of your meeting time is for the purpose of responding to God in prayer as a group. It is the idea that God has been speaking to you through the study of His Word, and now you will speak to Him in prayer. Though often overlooked, prayer is the first and most important application you can make about any study of the Word—to talk with God about what He is saying to you. In many ways, this final step is the real personal "application" for adults—not just something to do, but going to God and talking to Him about what He has said in His Word.

We sometimes trivialize the idea of application by trying to create artificial tasks or actions that we think will please God, meet His standards, or gain His approval. But God is not primarily concerned with these often superficial "sacrifices" of obedience. The offering He really desires from us is a "contrite heart" (Psalm 51:16-17). This step of supplication is simply opening our hearts to God—taking our needs, desires, failures, and hurts to Him and humbly asking Him to respond. This final part of your meeting is a time to pray to God as a group for one another, and for your group. It is a time to speak to God about what God has spoken to you.

## Tips for Guiding "Take It to Heart"

- Briefly remind your group about general prayer time guidelines: (1) Be brief: Keep requests and prayers short so everyone will have an opportunity to share and to pray; (2) Be relevant: Limit prayer requests to people and topics that are relevant to or known by the group; and (3) Be appropriate: Refrain from sharing personal details and stories about family or personal problems and conflicts that should remain confidential.

- Ask one of the moms to write down prayer requests, and then have her read all the requests out loud. If your group is comfortable praying, hearing the prayer requests will be enough to get praying. If your group is new, or some are not as confident praying, ask for a volunteer to pray for each individual request as the list is read. If time is short, ask two or three of the group members you know are comfortable with praying to pray, or you can just close in prayer yourself. Don't ever lecture or shame the group about prayer. Provide a model of prayer, and trust God to draw them out in His timing. Be flexible and gracious.

- Ask for a volunteer to open the prayer time, and let the group know that you will close the time of prayer. This will enable you to control when to end your group meeting time so it doesn't go too long. After closing with the "Amen," let your group members know that you will email the shared prayer requests to them, and encourage them to keep one another in prayer. Thank everyone for coming and let them know when and where the next group meeting is scheduled. If time allows, invite them to stay for refreshments and fellowship.

# HINTS: The Model

## Getting Your Group Talking

» **Introverts:** Introversion is not a personality weakness; it is a personality type designed by God with unique strengths and insights that your group needs. Extraverts tend to think out loud; introverts think "in quiet." It is not uncommon for extraverts to dominate discussions, so an introvert might have something insightful to add but will miss the opportunity because a verbal extravert has already moved the conversation in a different direction. As group leader, be sure to invite responses from introverts, and give them time to think out their thoughts (you might need to restrain the extraverts). Become aware of who are the introverts and extraverts in your group, as well as what your own personality type is and how you interact.

» **Discussion Questions:** As group leader, you will need to create discussion questions both ahead of time and on the fly. A good discussion question should be: simple (not complex or multifaceted), short (concise with minimal elaboration), sweet (not controversial), strategic (accomplishes a purpose for the meeting), and stimulating (enjoyable for everyone to talk about). A good discussion question should not be: closed (asking for a yes or no, right or wrong response), loaded (asked with a personal hidden agenda), rhetorical (asked with a desired outcome), or confusing (inviting moral or ethical ambiguity). Good questions will create good discussion.

» **Silence:** Most people will try to avoid silence, which can feel awkward and uncomfortable. However, silence can allow time for the Holy Spirit to work in hearts and minds. When the air goes dead in your group, gently suggest some lines of reflection or consideration to direct group members' thoughts, or ask a spiritually engaging question. Resist giving your own thoughts, and encourage the group to share theirs.

» **Leader Dependence:** Beware of unintentionally cultivating a dependence on yourself as the leader of the group for content and discussion. As a small group leader, the purpose of your preparation is not just to teach a lesson, but rather to facilitate a discussion. Since you will spend more time preparing the lesson, it will be natural for you to have a lot to say. However, a group can easily become dependent on you for discussion and insights. The more you allow that dependency to grow into a habit, the less the group will feel the need to interact. Teach when you need to, but always keep your main focus on facilitating and stimulating a discussion among your group members. They, not just you, are the life of your group.

» **Participation:** Invite your moms to become invested in the group by sharing in some of the regular responsibilities—bringing a snack or dessert; taking and organizing study and discussion notes for the group; recording prayer requests to email to the group; coming early to pray for the group. Giving others specific ways to be involved in the life of the group helps them feel it is "their" group and not just "her" (your) group. Ownership feeds participation.

» **Prayer Beginning:** The closing prayer time needs a clear beginning point. You can simply ask the question: "What is on your heart that we can pray about today?"

If the group is quiet, ask a specific member who might have a need that is known to the group, "How can we pray about [the need] for you today?"

» **Prayer Ending:** Even more important, though, the closing prayer time also needs a clear ending point. The easiest rule of group meeting etiquette to break is to not end on time. Going long in the closing prayer is probably the most common place to break the rule. It honors everyone in the group for you to end the meeting on time, so be ready to be the closer.

# Notes

# Section 6

# THE MENTOR

**The word "mentor" evokes thoughts of a formal position or posture of influence and accountability.** It can sound serious. And that's unfortunate. It's a great word, not just for what you are, but even more for what you do as a Mom Heart group leader. Here's a good dictionary definition: "A wise and trusted counselor or teacher." You provide a ministry of wisdom, counsel, and instruction for other mothers. In that sense, you are a "Mentor Mom" to them. It's not formal, but it is faith formational. And that's why you need to make sure you stay filled up with God's Spirit.

*I always wanted to be a hero—to sacrifice my life in a big way one time—and yet, God has required my sacrifice to be thousands of days, over many years, with one more kiss, one more story, one more meal.*

~*Desperate,* Sally Clarkson and Sarah Mae

# FEEDING YOUR MOM HEART GROUP

**Y**ou cannot offer living water to the mothers in your group if your own spiritual well is not filled up. This guide can equip you with practical skills to start, lead, and tend a group. However, those skills will not make you a spiritual life-giver. Only the Spirit of God, filling your own spirit, will enable you to encourage and influence other mothers in the Lord. As a mentor mom, you are a faith-forming influence on the moms who come to your Mom Heart group. Your life and faith will influence theirs. That kind of personal ministry needs to come from the overflow of a heart that is filled up with the Spirit of Christ.

The apostle John declared that Jesus is the Word, the *logos*, the full expression of all that God is. "And the Word became flesh, and dwelt among us, and we saw His glory, glory as of the only begotten from the Father, *full of grace and truth*" (John 1:14, italics added). John goes on to say, "the Law was given through Moses; *grace and truth* were realized through Jesus Christ" (1:17). We're no longer bound to the burdensome regulations of the Law of Moses to know God. Instead, we are now freed by grace and truth in Jesus to know God in our spirits. "For the law of the Spirit of life in Christ Jesus has set you free from the law of sin and death" (Romans 8:2)

All that Jesus was "full" of, we can now be filled with—the grace that brings us close to the merciful and loving God, and the truth that keeps us secure in our knowledge of Him. Now that we are, by faith, "in Christ" (see: Ephesians 1:3-14), we can live from the inside out—His grace and truth in our spirits working its way out in our lives. But that "inside-out" kind of life will happen only if we stay spiritually nourished by feeding our hearts and minds with His spiritual food—God's grace is food for the heart (or spirit), and God's truth is food for the mind. The more we stayed filled up with God's life, the more life we'll have to give to others.

> Only the Spirit of God, filling your own spirit, will enable you to encourage and influence other mothers in the Lord.

Whether you believe that you are a mentor or not, you will have a mentoring influence on the women in your Mom Heart group. You don't have to call yourself a "mentor mom," but you will be that to some degree in your group, not because of what the group leadership position brings to you, but because of what you bring to the position—a heart filled and overflowing with the grace and truth of God. How you relate to your moms, and what you share with them from your mom heart, will have a faith-forming influence on their lives. Whether you think you're a mentor or not, that is what a mentor does.

Following are some simple ways to think about how you can be a mentor and influencer, simply by making sure your stay spiritually nourished so that you'll have spiritual nourishment to offer to others.

## GRACE: Nourished by Prayers and People

Prayer is turning your spirit toward God to commune with Him. Prayer is arguably the most faith-affirming of the spiritual disciplines because through it you acknowledge you believe that God exists, that He listens, and that He will respond to you personally (see: Hebrews 11:6). Prayer opens your heart to the grace of God in a way nothing else can. In prayer, you experience His presence and His personal involvement in your life—the life of God intersecting your own life. You need the grace of His life living in your heart in order to serve the moms of your group. So, feed on God's grace in prayer.

In the same way that you can give God's grace to others, you can also receive God's grace for yourself. When you fellowship with other godly people who are feeding on God's grace in prayer, you are nourished by the overflow of their spirits, and your heart is spiritually encouraged and strengthened in their presence. Their faith feeds your faith, and fills your heart. Timothy received that same kind of grace from his friend and mentor Paul, and Paul had Barnabas, the "Son of Encouragement," to be a source of grace in his life. You need that grace in your life, too, so find a godly friend or mentor who will pray for you and encourage you, and make time to spend time with them. It will nourish your spirit.

## TRUTH: Nourished by the Word and Words

If prayer is you speaking to God, then reading His Word is God speaking to you. The truth of the Scripture is food for your mind—spiritual nourishment for growing in maturity, faith, and wisdom. There is "milk" for the immature believer, and there is "meat" for the mature (Hebrews 5:11-14). God's Word is "living and active" and goes deep into your "soul and spirit" (4:12). It is "inspired by God and profitable" for all that will make you mature (2 Timothy 3:16-17). It is God revealing His mind and heart to you, teaching you to be His follower, explaining spiritual realities, and guiding you with wisdom for life. You need His truth to teach others to follow Him. So, feed on God's truth in His Word.

In the same way that you learn from God by reading and studying His Word on your own, you also learn from others who feed on God's Word and then share what they learn in spoken messages and written books. Their insightful words can inspire, instruct, explain, explicate, and expand on the truths of God's Word in ways you might miss. When you listen to or read the words of others who study and think deeply about God's Word and the life of faith, you are nourished by the overflow of their maturity, wisdom, and insight—your mind is shaped and strengthened by their words. So, feed on God's truth in the messages, books, and writings of other godly believers you respect and trust.

You cannot offer living water to the mothers in your group if your own spiritual well is not filled up. You cannot be a faith-forming influence on others if your own faith is not being formed. Be sure you are being refreshed and nourished by God's grace and truth so you will be able to refresh and nourish others from His grace and truth.

The prophet Jeremiah witnessed God's judgment on Judah and Jerusalem in 586 B.C. Those left behind had reason to feel hopeless, yet in the aftermath of the defeat and destruction, Jeremiah could still declare to the people of Judah: "This I recall to my mind, therefore I have hope. The LORD's lovingkindnesses indeed never cease, for His compassions never fail. They are new every morning; Great is Your faithfulness. 'The LORD is my portion,' says my soul, 'Therefore I have hope in Him'" (Lamentations 3:21-224).

There are many reasons that moms can come to your Mom Heart group feeling defeated, depressed, and without hope. Life can be hard, and hope can be fleeting. But you have the opportunity to be a mentor-like Jeremiah to your moms—to declare God's love, faithfulness, and mercy, and to remind them that our hope is in Christ and in the faithfulness of God. That word of hope must come from a heart that, like Jeremiah's, has recalled to mind, every morning, the blessings and provisions of God. The grace and truth that you bring to your moms' hearts will give them the hope they need to be faithful.

> You cannot offer living water to the mothers in your group if your own spiritual well is not filled up.

# HINTS: THE MENTOR

## Giving from a Full Spirit

» **Family:** It should be self-evident, but sadly too often it isn't—if your life at home is out of order, then your spiritual life will be out of order. You can't give from a full spirit if your heart is divided and distracted by unresolved stress or discord at home. Be honest with yourself and your group about the state of your heart.

» **Place at Home:** Be sure to have your own personal space at home where you can retreat for times of quiet and spiritual refreshment, if only for a few minutes. Create a "mom's place" with things that minister to your spirit—comfy chair, special books, your music, lighted candles, lovely pictures, living plants.

» **Get Away:** Different personalities will retreat in different ways, but the idea of getting away is biblical and basic. We need to separate ourselves occasionally from media, daily routines, distractions, and everything else that keeps us from focusing on our own emotional and physical needs and spiritual health. And yes, we can even need time away from people. Plan a weekend getaway however often you need to in order to tend to the needs of your spirit.

» **Worship:** Music is processed in a different part of the brain. If music is the language of worship, then we need to be training that part of our brain with good music. Perhaps we are learning the language of eternity. There is a mysterious but very real effect that music has on the spirit by God's design, so feed your spirit with music regularly.

» **Self-Acceptance:** If you cannot accept yourself as God has made you, then you stand to miss much of the Spirit's work and leading in your life. Learning to "love ... yourself" is part of your spiritual nature. God accepts you unconditionally, and wants to use you just as you are. This may be an important part of accepting the ministry God has given to you as a mentoring mom.

# Notes

# Section 7

# THE MISSION

**Every movement has a mission.** A simple dictionary definition of a mission is: "An important goal or purpose that is accompanied by strong conviction." There is a clear understanding of where the movement is going and how it will get there. A Mom Heart group movement has a simple mission at its heart: to reach more moms and grow more groups. A group that cannot see beyond itself is not a group "on a mission from God." We want part of the identity of being in a Mom Heart group to be a sense of mission.

The task of building our homes into places of beauty and life that will feed the hearts, souls, and minds of our children is the most comprehensive task to which God has called us as mothers. We are called quite literally to be "home makers"—to plan and shape a home environment that provides our families with both a safe resting place and a launching pad for everything they do in the world.

~*The Mission of Motherhood,* Sally Clarkson

# Growing Your Mom Heart Group

Growth takes time. Jesus' model for discipleship was intentional, relational, and patient. He intentionally invested in the lives of a handful of disciples who went out and invested relationally in the lives of others. The growth of Jesus' ministry did not happen overnight, and you should not expect quick growth for your group either. Be patient, but move forward with intentional purpose to grow your Mom Heart group. God is looking for your faithfulness, not your fruitfulness. Fruitfulness always follows faithfulness.

Your priority as a leader should never be only to pursue growth in numbers. The number of moms involved in your group or ministry can certainly indicate a healthy and thriving group, but it should not become an artificial or counterfeit measure of success that tempts you to place your confidence as a leader in the wrong indicator. Your priority should be growth in Christ—to build up your moms in the Lord and help them grow in spiritual maturity. And yet even that is not the end purpose of your group.

If the Spirit of God is a river of living water flowing into the life of your group, it is meant to flow in you, through you, and then out to others. If it all goes in but then nothing flows out, your group can eventually become stagnant, and no longer living or growing. The ultimate purpose of your group is not just to grow, but to grow out and reach other women. That's the kind of biblical growth that will make a difference—growth in spiritual maturity expressed in a heart for reaching out to others.

> God is looking for your faithfulness, not your fruitfulness. Be patient, but move forward with intentional purpose to grow your Mom Heart group. God is looking for your faithfulness, not your fruitfulness.

Look at the list of possible kinds of Mom Heart groups again in Section 1. There are many mothers in the body of Christ and in your community who are minimalized, marginalized, and even neglected. They need the hope and encouragement that you are finding in your group. If you are growing in Christ, then you have truth and grace to offer other mothers who are thirsty. When you do that as a group, united in purpose and motivated by love for Christ and others, you will show the world that you are His disciples. Here's an acrostic that summarizes this kind of vision for your GROUP:

# Go Reach Others Uniting in Purpose.

## Sharpen the Vision of Your Group

It's easy for a group to settle into a routine, and to become comfortable and complacent just doing what they've always done. When that happens, vision dims and dulls for what God's larger purpose is for your group. To keep vision for your group sharp, take some time every quarter to talk about your bigger mission as a group. Use the GROUP acrostic below to evaluate together if there are ways you can become more outreaching.

# G – Go: Initiate

Don't wait for moms to approach you! Prayerfully consider moms you know who may be interested in your group, or need to be in a Mom Heart group, and then take the initiative to go and seek them out. Depending on the size and nature of your group, you can invite them to join your group, or even start a new one for them. You may be motivated, and even gifted, to minister to mothers, but it won't happen until you go, until you initiate.

# R – Reach: Invite

Some women won't respond to a general announcement about a group. Perhaps they feel they're too busy, or they're insecure about responding to a stranger, or they just don't want to risk rejection, or they don't feel worthy to be in the group. Whatever the reason, when you reach out personally, it tells them that you're interested in them and that they're welcome in your group. Sometimes all someone needs is to be asked!

# O – Others: Include

There can be an appropriate time for an exclusive group–if you're limited in size; if it's a special needs group; when you are building strategically into the lives of a few committed women; or other special situations. However, always keep in mind that God's kingdom is inclusive–it is offered to all who will come to Christ. Being biblically inclusive as a group means always looking out for others who need to be included, to invite them in or to help them find a group.

# U – Uniting in: Inspire

History has been changed by small groups of people united in a common purpose and inspired by a shared vision. You may not change history, but you can change the lives of many mothers through your small group. The mothers you inspire will go on to touch their own families, and other mothers. Always communicate a higher vision for your group, then let the Spirit unite you in reaching for it. You are inspiring eternity-changers.

# P – Purpose: Influence

Every day, women are fed a steady diet of half-truths and even lies about motherhood by the prevailing culture. What they hear is rarely, if ever, biblical, affirming, or visionary. But you can influence other mothers with biblical truth about God's heart, design, and purpose for motherhood. You have the opportunity to influence other women by helping them find eternal purpose and meaning in their lives at home. Your influence is purposeful and powerful.

## Broaden the Vision for Your Group

Never before in the history of the world have we been able to connect and communicate instantly and personally with people all around the world. We take the Internet for granted now, but to generations before us the idea would have seemed in the realm of the miraculous. Though it certainly has its downsides, the world is different now because of the wonders of connectedness the Internet has introduced.

> No matter what the country, culture, time, or place, we believe that a mission that can reach mothers is reaching the "heart" of a culture.

As we consider how God might use Mom Heart groups for His kingdom, we cannot ignore the mission of the church to go into all the world (Matthew 28:18-20). As former missionaries in Western and Eastern Europe, we have long thought that mothers are an under-served part of the world mission vision. We believe they are a doorway into families and communities. When you reach a mom's heart, you also reach fathers, children, neighbors, and generations. No matter what the country, culture, time, or place, we believe that a mission that can reach mothers is reaching the "heart" of a culture.

Mothers are generally more available, and through their children they generally have many relationships with other mothers in their communities. In their homes, depending upon the culture, they exercise a strong and lasting influence over the hearts, values, and beliefs of their children. That is not to minimize the impact and influence of fathers on the family, but the potential impact of mothers should never be marginalized or underestimated. By God's design, mothers are uniquely suited and situated to shape the spiritual atmosphere of their homes.

That's why part of our mission vision for Mom Heart is to see Mom Heart groups starting in other countries—first in English-speaking nations, and then through translated materials in non-English-speaking nations. It will be a long, slow process, but that is part of our long term vision for Mom Heart Ministry. And we want to make Mom Heart groups in America an integral part of that vision through the Internet.

MomHeart.com is the online home for Mom Heart Ministry. It is where we can provide resources to encourage and equip mothers to start, lead, and tend Mom Heart groups not just in our country, but around the world. As that happens, our plan is to find ways to spotlight and connect with those Mom Heart groups. We want to profile groups in Europe, Australia, South Africa, Indonesia, China, South America, and wherever God brings moms together to strengthen their mom hearts. But even more, we want to see groups here connecting with groups in other countries—moms encouraging moms through the Internet around the world. It's a "vision that is yet for the appointed time" that we believe "will certainly come" (Habakkuk 2:3).

Don't neglect the mission of your Mom Heart group—neither the local mission to reach out to moms right where you are, nor the global mission to reach out to moms around the world. Jesus instructed us not to be distracted and worried about all the daily vicissitudes and needs of life. Rather, He commanded us to "seek first His kingdom and His righteousness" (Matthew 6:33a). In other words, sharpen your vision to see what God is doing in the world to build and expand His Kingdom, and pursue that. It's easy to become "nearsighted" in our vision, seeing only what is near to us. You can help your Mom Heart group correct their vision to bring into clear focus what God can do through mothers, not just in your community, but around the world. That's a vision worth seeing ... and seeking.

# HINTS: The Mission

## Thinking About Growing

» **Initiate:** Women attending your Mom Heart group will likely represent a variety of cultural backgrounds from within your community. Sometimes you may need to wear your "brave face" to initiate conversations with moms in many settings—swim lessons, soccer practice, on Facebook, at church, and even when buying school supplies and materials. Just step out in faith.

» **Invite:** The women who become a part of your group will probably mention how grateful they are that you stepped out of your comfort zone to initiate a conversation and invite them to your group. Not many others will. Just ask.

» **Include:** Be aware of women who might be marginalized or minimalized and reach out to include them in your group. Look for "mom hearts" that need to be encouraged and helped. You will be touching the life of a woman who is giving life to the next generation.

» **Inspire:** With no support from culture, or even from churches at times, many Christian moms have lost their heart for biblical motherhood. You have the opportunity to inspire them with hope that God's design for motherhood is a divine calling with eternal purpose and spiritual blessing.

» **Influence:** Many women are gifted and motivated, but not so many possess spiritual confidence or feel the personal freedom as a woman to exercise the gifts of influence they have from God. If you are that mom, know that it's OK for you to own your own influence, and to exercise that influence by faith with God's direction. After all, it's His influence.

# Notes

# Section 8
# THE MESSAGE

**Every movement has a message.** It's what defines it, gives it direction, and makes it distinct from other movements. There are, of course, competing messages about biblical motherhood—they can create confusion for Christian moms, leading them off in search of God's truth that too often can leave them feeling either trapped by what they find, or lost and without direction. However, we believe that the beliefs that shape Mom Heart are biblically sound, reflect the true heart of God for mothers, and will give moms a sense of freedom and direction. Our message is what makes us Mom Heart.

Seeing my children develop a heart for God's service and begin to find their own place of ministry in the world is a reachable goal for me as a mother, because God has designed me to fulfill this purpose. This is the true ministry of motherhood—to usher my children into the living presence of God, to nurture in them a heart for Jesus and the Great Commission he has called each of us to fulfill.

~*The Ministry of Motherhood,* Sally Clarkson

# Teaching Your Mom Heart Group

Mom Heart teaches a distinct biblical message about God's heart for motherhood. However, the distinctiveness of our message about motherhood is not just in the details of what we believe, but also in how we teach the scriptures that teach about motherhood. We don't come to Scripture intent on making all of the mom passages fit into a box, whether our own or someone else's. Not every theological box is necessarily bad, but when Scripture does not create it, the unfortunate result is too often what we call "Christian law," or legalism. Boxed-up ideas for motherhood become rules that must be followed—if you're not in the box, you're out of God's will. We believe God is bigger than our boxes.

We come to the Scriptures together to listen for God's heart in a personal letter written by Him to His people, not to cut and paste bits of truth to fit into a manmade

> One of the most loving things you can do is to teach the moms in your group in a way that helps them find the message of grace and freedom in Christ, and the confidence of biblical motherhood that God designed them to enjoy.

doctrinal box. The purpose of a Mom Heart group is to open God's Word with a spirit of humility and discernment to hear what the Spirit has to say about motherhood and the Christian life. As a Mom Heart group leader and teacher you are following the example of Jesus who taught with "grace and truth," not with law (John 1:17).

> Grace is at the heart of teaching the moms in your group. You are freeing them from counterfeit and burdensome views of motherhood that cannot fulfill their longing to be the mom that God designed them to be.

Grace is at the heart of teaching the moms in your group. You are freeing them from counterfeit and burdensome views of motherhood that cannot fulfill their longing to be the mom that God designed them to be. You are helping them find the blessing, purpose, and sense of fulfillment that God intended for them as a mom in His divine design for motherhood. One of the most loving things you can do is to teach the moms in your group in a way that helps them find the message of grace and freedom in Christ, and the confidence of biblical motherhood that God designed them to enjoy.

There is not the space in this short book to survey all of the texts about motherhood that shape what we believe at Mom Heart. However, we have listed a few below. Our hope is that these few texts will help you embrace the spirit of grace and discernment that we encourage for group studies.

## Titus 2:3-5 – The Mom Heart of Old and Young

This familiar passage should be at the heart of every

biblically-informed ministry to mothers. The Apostle Paul is writing to his close friend and faithful fellow-worker Titus, instructing him to entrust the teaching and training of young mothers in the church to the "older women." The term "older" naturally refers to being advanced in age, but it also can refer to being older in relative terms. The context of the passage indicates faithful mothers who are old enough to have proven themselves to be mature and trustworthy. It is not about defining when that occurs, but about understanding the spirit of the ministry that Paul was describing.

> Older women likewise are to be reverent in their behavior, not malicious gossips nor enslaved to much wine, teaching what is good, so that they may encourage the young women to love their husbands, to love their children, to be sensible, pure, workers at home, kind, being subject to their own husbands, so that the word of God will not be dishonored. (Titus 2:3-5)

Paul's instructions are in two parts. First, he describes five qualities of the "older women" that will qualify them to teach the younger. Then, he describes seven kinds of lessons they are to teach to the "young women." In both cases, Paul's lists are not meant to be comprehensive, but rather representative. He is describing lives to emulate, and suggesting lessons to imitate, but not creating rules to regulate. It's about the spirit, not the law.

☐ **The Older Woman: Qualities of a Teacher (2:3-4a)**

Paul describes this older woman as "reverent," choosing a

term used only here in the Bible that suggests she is fulfilling a priestly role. Within an irreverent and ungodly culture, Paul calls the older women of the church in Crete to stand apart as God's representatives to the younger women living in and coming out of that culture. The older woman's behavior should befit whatever God considers sacred, which in this case seems to be their role as older women. In addition to that spiritual quality, Paul says that the older woman should also be known for four other specific traits.

> Paul's profile of an older woman in first-century Crete has lost nothing in the translation of two thousand years. As a Mom Heart group leader and teacher, the qualities Paul describes will qualify you to be an effective minister to other moms, whatever your age.

First, the older woman must be self-controlled in her words and attitudes, not a "malicious gossip." Paul uses an unusually strong term, *diabolos*, that is used mostly of Satan ("devil") and means here to slander or accuse falsely (he alone also uses the term this way here and in 1 and 2 Timothy). Second, she is to be self-controlled in her desires and habits, "not enslaved to much wine." By inference, she is to restrain her desires and impulses not just for wine but for anything else that would belie her testimony of godliness. Third, she is known as one who teaches what is good (literally, a good-teacher). The kind of goodness referred to here suggests teaching things that are beautiful, noble, and praiseworthy. Fourth, her teaching should be known to "encourage" or admonish others. In English, we might say that she "sensibilizes" the young women—she helps them come to their senses.

Paul's profile of an older woman in first-century Crete has

lost nothing in the translation of two thousand years. As a Mom Heart group leader and teacher, the qualities Paul describes will qualify you to be an effective minister to other moms, whatever your age. Ask yourself the following questions and ask God to help you embody the spirit of the older woman:

- Am I willing to be God's representative in my personal ministry to the women in my Mom Heart group?

- Am I self-controlled in my words and attitudes, refusing to engage in gossip and slander?

- Am I self-controlled in my desires and habits, not enslaved to anything that would detract from my ministry for God?

- Am I committed to being a teacher of what is good—of God's truth that is beautiful, noble, and praiseworthy?

- Am I a committed to being a teacher of sensible living— of God's truth that encourages faithfulness, soundness, and stability?

## ☐ The Young Woman: Lessons for a Teacher (2:4b-5)

Paul does not profile the "young women" as he did the older, but rather describes seven lessons the young moms need to hear and learn from the older mothers. These lessons are obviously about qualities that the older women have already acquired, which is why they are qualified to teach them. So these are qualities for every woman, and every mother. Paul says that the purpose of learning these qualities is about much more than just becoming a better woman, wife, and mother; it is "so that the word of God will not be dishonored." Teaching and embodying these qualities helps preserve the integrity and honor of the Scriptures that you are teaching.

Answer the questions below about how you personally can grow in each quality as a godly woman, and help those in your Mom Heart group to grow in each quality as godly young women.

- "Love their husbands" (literally, husband-lovers) – How am I, every day, choosing to love and prefer my God-provided husband? How can I encourage younger moms to practice loving and enjoying their husbands.

- "Love their children" (literally, child-lovers) – How am I, every day, choosing to love and prefer my God-given children? How can I encourage younger moms to develop loving attitudes and words of grace for their children?

- "Sensible" – How am I becoming sound-minded and self-controlled, curbing my desires and impulses in order to live sensibly? How can I encourage younger moms to think sensibly and biblically about their choices in life?

- "Pure" – How am I choosing reverent and sacred thoughts and desires over worldly and impure ones so I will have a testimony of purity? How can I encourage younger moms to maintain purity in their thoughts and choices?

- "Workers at home" (literally, home-guards) – How am I guarding and keeping watch over my home domain and all who live within it? How can I encourage younger moms to value and cultivate the home domain God has entrusted to them?

- "Kind" – How am I exercising God's kindness toward my family members, and toward others, so I will have a testimony of goodness? How can I encourage younger moms to let kindness, a fruit of the Spirit, guard their thoughts and words?

- "Subject to their own husbands" – How am I honoring and respecting my husband in our marriage, family, and lives together? How can I encourage younger moms to cultivate biblical attitudes and desires toward their husbands?

## Luke 1:26–2:20 – The Mom Heart of Mary

The story of Jesus' birth cannot be told without the story of Mary. In Luke's narrative, there is much to learn from the heart of the woman God chose to be the mother of Jesus. Even though she was very young, perhaps only about fourteen when visited by the angel Gabriel, it is evident that God had uniquely prepared her to be the mother of the "Son of God." Consider some of the qualities she exhibited as recorded in Luke's account.

**Confidence (1:26-30, 34)** – Mary was not fearful or reactionary to the visit by Gabriel. She was "perplexed" by his unusual greeting which addressed her as "favored one," but she continued to listen carefully. She confidently questioned the angel's announcement that she would conceive and bear a son asking, "How can this be, since I am a virgin?" She did not doubt the angel's words, but simply asked how what he was describing would happen.

**Trust (1:31-38)** – Gabriel told Mary that she would conceive as a virgin by the power of the Holy Spirit and bear a son, Jesus, who would be the Son of God and the King of Israel. When Gabriel assured her that "nothing is impossible with God," Mary's response affirmed that she believed it as well: "Behold, the bondslave of the Lord; may it be done to me according to your word." She expressed complete trust in God, without fear, doubt, or denial. She was a servant of God, and she trusted Him and His messenger.

**Boldness (1:39-40)** – After Gabriel's visit, Mary went "in a hurry" to visit her relative Elizabeth, who was also pregnant. However, the hill country of Judah was a long way south of Nazareth, and the trip would take up to five days, so this was not a small journey for a young girl. She likely had a family escort, or joined a caravan going in that direction, but it was a significant journey that she made there and back without hesitation.

**Knowledge of Scripture (1:46-55)** – When Elizabeth greeted Mary with a blessing for her and the child she was carrying, Mary responded with a personal song of exultation from numerous scriptures. What her "Magnificat" reveals is a heart so full of God's Word that her song flowed naturally and spontaneously from her Spirit. In her brief fourteen years, her life obviously had been steeped in Scripture. Whether at home or in the temple or synagogue, Mary had listened and internalized the Scriptures she had heard.

**Adaptable (2:7)** – The conditions surrounding the actual birth of Jesus suggest that Mary was flexible and adaptable when confronted with change. Joseph likely owned a house in Bethlehem, but when they arrived the "guest room" (NIV; often translated "inn") attached to the house was already full due to the census. So they possibly shared the larger main room. When the time came for the birth, Mary laid the baby Jesus in a "manger," or feeding trough, that was cut into the floor of the house at the end where they kept the animals. She simply adapted to her changing living conditions.

**A Mother's Heart (2:19, 51)** – Luke provides a brief glimpse into Mary's heart when he recounts the shepherds leaving after their visit to the Christ child. They had come to tell about their angelic visitors announcing the birth of "a Savior, who is Christ the Lord." Luke records that "Mary treasured all these things, pondering them in her heart." Mary's heart was focused on what God was doing in the life of her child. When Jesus was twelve and entering manhood, Luke repeats those same words about Mary (1:51). Her "mom heart" was tuned in to God at work in her life and in the life of her child.

**Kept Traditions (2:21-24)** – Mary and Joseph followed the Jewish laws and traditions, taking Jesus to the temple in Jerusalem to "present Him to the Lord," and to offer a sacrifice according to the "Law of the Lord." Jesus would grow up with parents who honored and acknowledged God in their home through the Jewish feasts and traditions that celebrated His faithfulness and sovereignty.

All of these qualities of Mary's motherhood are anecdotal observations, but they provide a glimpse into the heart of the mother God chose for Jesus. Use the qualities to examine your own heart: How are you confident as a mother? How can you trust God with your children? Are you bold when you need to be? Are you hiding the Scriptures deep in your heart? Can you be flexible and adaptable when you need to be? Are you treasuring and pondering in your heart the things that God is doing in your child's life? Are you creating a stable home with traditions that honor and acknowledge God's reality and faithfulness?

## 1 Thessalonians 2:7-8 – The Mom Heart of Paul

The apostle Paul had a clear view of the role of motherhood in the life of the home and church, which is evident in his instructions in Titus 2:3-5. However, he also provides a very brief glimpse into his thoughts about motherhood when comparing his ministry in the Thessalonian church to a nursing mother's concern for her child. He draws on an image used numerous times throughout Scripture to describe God's relationship to His people.

> Is your own mom heart characterized by gentleness, tenderness, and affection toward your child?

First, Paul compares his ministry to the "gentleness" that a nursing mother shows to her baby. Paul often mentions gentleness in his letters, which is a fruit of the Spirit (Galatians 5:23). Second, Paul compares his ministry to how a mother "tenderly cares for her own children." There is a sense of tender kindness and protection suggested by his words. Finally, Paul compares his motivation toward the church to the "affection" that a mother feels toward her child. He uses an unusual term that suggests an intense desire and longing love. These qualities, though anecdotal and directed toward the church, are nonetheless examples of how Paul envisioned the heart of a mother toward her child. Is your own mom heart characterized by gentleness, tenderness, and affection toward your child?

## GENESIS 1–3 – The Mom Heart of God

To get to the heart of what the Bible says about motherhood, though, we have to get into the heart of God. What is God's heart for motherhood? Though there are no divine statements in Scripture that directly answer that question, there is one place where God's intentions can be discerned—in the creation account of Genesis.

> We want to help moms discover the mom heart of God, and the divine design He intended "from the beginning" for motherhood.

In the first three chapters of Genesis, there are intimations and clues about God's heart for motherhood in his design for mankind. Before the man and woman fall into sin, God creates them and gives them their mandate, so insights that can be discerned are from a time of purity and innocence. Nothing would ever be the same after the events of Genesis chapter three, but God's ideals and eternal purposes for motherhood were fully engaged in chapters one and two. That's where we can look to find the heart of God toward mothers.

There seven general principles drawn from the narrative of Genesis that help to define what it means to have a "mom heart." Though sin has distorted everything, we can still aspire to the ideals of God. That is what we mean when we say we want to "restore moms' hearts to God's heart for motherhood." We want to help moms discover the mom heart of God, and the divine design He intended "from the beginning" for motherhood. Here are seven qualities of a mom heart drawn from Genesis 1-3.

## 1. It's a Heart that Bears the Image of God (1:26-27)

> God created man in His own image, in the image of God
> He created him, male and female He created them.

The first quality of God's mom heart is His divine fingerprint—the fact that every mother bears the image of God, and her children bear the image the God. Motherhood is not just a burdensome task to be done, but an expression of the very nature of God himself. The image of God that each mother bears, though distorted now by sin, nonetheless makes every act of motherhood deeply meaningful, spiritually strategic, and eternally significant. God's image in her— His sovereign, creative, relational, and moral qualities—is poured into all of the activities and responsibilities given to her domain. The choices a mother makes in her home and family are expressions of who God is and what He values. God designed her to flesh out, or incarnate, for her children what He is like and values.

## 2. It's a Heart that Values Having Children (1:28)

> God blessed them; and God said to them, "Be
> fruitful and multiply, and fill the earth ..."

The second quality of God's mom heart is a mother's heart for her children, and the understanding that God greatly values children. In His eternal plan, children are God's primary means for populating the earth with righteous generations and creating a people who follow and worship him. Each child is a "blessing" from God to parents (Psalm 127:3-5), and His heart is pleased to see a mother loving her children and understanding that she is blessed by them, not burdened by them. The purest essence of biblical motherhood is a heart for children. The love of a mother in God's divine design is an irreplaceable influence on a child's heart, dreams, self-image, and potential.

## 3. It's a Heart that Believes in the Family (1:28, 2:24)

> God blessed them ... For this reason a man shall leave his
> father and his mother, and be joined to his wife; and
> they shall become one flesh.

The third quality of God's mom heart is a heart for family. God gave authority to the first family to "rule over" His creation. His first communication with the new family, Adam and Eve, was to delegate stewardship of the new creation to them. Together they were given the mandate to fill, subdue, and bring order to the world. Family is critical to God's eternal plan of redemption—it pictures God's involvement in our lives through family-based analogies and metaphors, and it is the primary influence in the spiritual formation of children. God designed a mother to help her family exercise their stewardship over creation together.

## 4. It's a Heart that Works to Subdue the Home (1:28)

> ...and God said to them, "Be fruitful and
> multiply, and fill the earth, and subdue it ..."

The fourth quality of God's mom heart is a heart for the home. God gave the woman He had created a co-conservatorship with her husband over the earth. Her primary "domain" to rule over and subdue would be her home and children. A mother cannot build a strong home, and influence her children spiritually, unless she values her home and her role in it. Subduing a home is not just about managing the physical environment, but also about cultivating the spiritual and relational atmosphere where children are loved, instructed, inspired, encouraged, directed, and helped in the Lord. Home is where the heart of motherhood lives.

## 5. It's a Heart that Looks for God's Blessing (1:28, 31)

> God blessed them ... God saw all that He
> had made, and behold, it was very good.

The fifth quality of God's mom heart is a heart that looks for and expects God's blessing. God blessed Adam and Eve, and declared the first family He created to be "very good." The mother who looks for God's blessings on her and her husband, and on her children, will bring the Spirit of God into her home. It is an acknowledgment to her children that she believes that God exists, and is present,

> A mother cannot build a strong home, and influence her children spiritually, unless she values her home and her role in it.

good, and involved. Her expectation of blessing is a powerful testimony of faith that helps her children understand and receive God's blessing.

## 6. It's a Heart that Wants to Be a Helper (2:29–31)

> Then the Lord God said, "It is not good for the man to be alone; I will make him a helper suitable for him ..."

The sixth quality of God's mom heart is a heart that seeks to be a godly wife and helper. There is no mom without a dad in God's plan, so marriage is a critical part of a mom heart. God made the woman to be Adam's "helper" because he was alone; she was "suitable" to Adam because she was like him and "obviously" not like the animals. God made a companion for Adam. The mutual call of a husband and wife to serve God together gives meaning to the purpose of family. This modeling of love, help, and mutual service is critical to the health of her marriage and family, and to her children's growth toward maturity and wholeness.

## 7. It's a Heart that Seeks to Give Life (3:20)

> Now the man called his wife's name Eve,
> because she was the mother of all the living.

The seventh quality of God's mom heart is an understanding of what it means to be a "life-giver." A mother gives physical life to her children, but she also gives them existential life—a strong emotional life through her relationship with them, a deep spiritual life through biblical instruction and personal faith, and a rich cultural life though the nurturing of beauty, order, and meaningful traditions in her home. A life-giving mother is energized by the life of God's Spirit within her, both inside and outside her home. She values truth, goodness, and beauty in all their expressions because they are channels of God's life and grace.

# PSALM 127:3 – Your Mom Heart

> Behold, children are a gift of the Lord, the
> fruit of the womb is a reward.

Many Christian mothers today are confused and directionless in their search for meaning as a mother. Motherhood seems to them just an incidental part of marriage that needs to be planned, managed, and too often endured. They have lost sight of their place as a mother in the grand story of God's redemption of his fallen creation. When we read in English that children are a "gift" from the Lord, we naturally think of an undeserved present. But in Hebrew, that

122

word consistently means throughout the Old Testament an inheritance or possession. The psalmist is saying that children are the portion of God's inheritance given to us to wisely steward as our priceless and prized possession. Similarly, a "reward" was wages paid for work done. The blessings of parenthood are a kind of payment from God for raising those children in the Lord. That is the picture we often miss.

As a Mom Heart group leader, you can help a new generation of mothers discover God's mom heart—the eternal principles of motherhood that bring the greatest benefit and blessing not just to mothers and children, but to future generations of godly descendants, to your family and community culture, and even to civilization. You can help a mother find her place as an integral and strategic part of God's plan of redemption.

> The simplest expression of what it means to have a mom heart is a personal affirmation of Psalm 127:3—that you believe that your children are a gift from God, and a reward in this life.

Your role as a Mom Heart group leader and teacher begins with your own mom heart. The simplest expression of what it means to have a mom heart is a personal affirmation of Psalm 127:3—that you believe that your children are a gift from God, and a reward in this life. If that is your starting point, then it will take you naturally to wanting to help other mothers find that "mom heart" from God. That is how you can truly love your Mom Heart group, by helping each mother find and strengthen their own mom heart.

# HINTS: The Message

## Teaching for the Heart

» **Devotional Journal:** Start a devotional journal to accompany your regular devotional Bible reading and study. Choose a leather or hardbound journal to make it special. On the title page, give it a name, such as "My Mom Heart Journal" or "My Mom-Word Memoir" or a name you create. Handwrite the title and decorate the page with as much artistic flair as you care to add (be sure to add your name, children's names, and date for the benefit of future generations). As you read the Scriptures in your regular devotions, become aware of passages that either directly or indirectly speak to you about God's heart or your heart for motherhood, and about children and parenting. When you come across a passage that you think belongs in the journal, do the following: (1) start on a new page; (2) write out a summary or descriptive title of some kind for the passage; (3) write out the full Scripture reference location of the passage (e.g., Psalms 127:3); (4) write out the full Bible passage (or a portion of it); and (5) then journal your own thoughts as a mother of how the passage speaks to you. If you like, (6) include a short written prayer at the end. Your journal can be a lifelong project that will strengthen your mom heart, and a legacy of faith that you will leave to your children and their children.

» **Be Sharpened:** Ask a co-leader, a mom in your group, or someone outside of your group to be your "Sharpen-Her." This is not an accountability relationship, but rather a "recountability" relationship. Here's the concept: When you find a Scripture that speaks to you in some way, especially one you think you might want to teach in your group, you simply "recount" that passage and your thoughts about it to your Sharpen-Her by email or message. You don't have to say "May I ..." or engage in small talk first, because she will know why you're sending it to her. She will simply respond back to you with her own thoughts and insights about the passage and your comments. It's a modern expression of Proverbs 27:17, "As iron sharpens iron, so a person sharpens his friend" (NET). Your sharpen-her is not necessarily your BFF, although she could be, but rather a seasoned friend or mentor whose spiritual maturity and biblical insight you respect and trust.

» **Mom Heart Massage:** If you can work it into your Mom Heart group schedule, set aside one or more meetings just to review the passages mentioned in this chapter, or others that deal directly with God's design for motherhood. We all need to be reminded about the things we think we know, but that we too easily forget to remember. If there's pushback from your group because they don't want to cover old group, you can always quote Peter: "Therefore, I will always be ready to remind you of these things, even though you already know them, and have been established in the truth which is present with you. I consider it right, as long as I am in this earthly dwelling, to stir you up by way of reminder ..." (2 Peter 1:12-13). If you think the group needs a refresher on God's heart for motherhood, go with your heart.

# Notes

_____

_____

_____

_____

_____

_____

_____

_____

_____

_____

_____

_____

_____

_____

_____

_____

_____

_____

_____

_____

# Section 9
# THE METHODS

**Whether you think of yourself as a "teacher" or not, as a Mom Heart group leader you are in a teaching role.** Because you will study the Scriptures for the lessons, and lead the discussions, you will have information and insights to impart to those in your group. But Mom Heart is about more than just passing on knowledge. There is a core understanding about motherhood, faith, grace, and truth behind the instruction that must inform and shape what is taught in a group. The methods you follow will shape your group.

If we don't take personal responsibility to train and disciple our children and to teach them that they are responsible to teach others, then the battle for our children's souls and minds will be lost—and the battle will go badly for this generation. One of the greatest works we will ever do is to light the fire in our children's hearts for becoming kingdom workers.

*~The Mom Walk,* Sally Clarkson

# SHAPING YOUR MOM HEART GROUP

**M**any small groups for moms probably start with the vision of getting out of the house and getting together for mutual support and fellowship. That very natural impetus has created "Mom's Day Out" ministries everywhere you turn. And in the thick of raising young children at home, that is understandably a very appealing idea. However, moms need more than an MDO to keep going.

Your role as a group leader is about much more than just facilitating fellowship; it is also about preserving and passing on God's truth to other moms that can change lives and affect eternity. The same conviction that drives you to teach your children the truths they need for life should also drive you to take your role as a Mom Heart group leader and teacher just as seriously. It's the same conviction that drove the apostles as they started the church after Jesus left them. It's the same conviction, driven by the same scriptures, that continues to grow the church today. The biblical methods for expressing those convictions have remained the same since Jesus gave us our marching orders as His disciples.

Some moms are ready and eager to enter the battle for moms' hearts and minds. Others are cautiously confident and willing to consider giving it a go. Others are emotionally resistant, thinking they are neither qualified nor gifted to actually teach. Whichever mom you are, here's the reality for everyone: Being a Mom Heart group leader and teacher is not just about what you think you can or should do for God; it is about what God says he can and will do through you. If you are a woman of God who is faithful and available, He can and will use you.

> Being a Mom Heart group leader and teacher is not just about what you think you can or should do for God; it is about what God says he can and will do through you.

There are a few key passages of Scripture that have shaped the growth of the church for two thousand years. They have shaped our own family commitment to personal ministry for four decades, and now feed our vision for a movement of Mom Heart groups. This short handbook does not allow for an in-depth study of each passage, but you can glean from them the larger principles what God wants you to know about the biblical methods that shape this ministry, and can shape yours, too. God wants to use you to make a difference in the lives of other moms. These passages are speaking to you, not to "someone else." You can gain confidence from His Word to be the teacher that He has prepared you to be.

## God Wants You to Make Disciples
### MATTHEW 28:18-20 (ACTS 1:7-8)

All ministry in Christ's name—in every place to everyone of any time—begins with the final words of Jesus that end Matthew's gospel:

All authority has been given to Me in heaven and on earth. Go therefore and make disciples of all the nations, baptizing them in the name of the Father and the Son and the Holy Spirit, teaching them to observe all that I commanded you; and lo, I am with you always, even to the end of the age. (Matthew 28:18-20)

For forty days after His resurrection, Jesus appeared to His followers and instructed His apostles about the kingdom of God (see Acts 1:1-9). At the end of that time, He gathered His apostles together to let them know that they would soon "receive power when the Holy Spirit has come upon you" (1:9) and that they would become His "witnesses" not just in Israel but in all the earth. In His final words before ascending into heaven Jesus commanded them to "make disciples of all the nations" (Matthew 28:19), assuring them that He would be with them "always" through His Spirit (see John 14:16-17f).

Jesus' one simple command to "make disciples," carried forward by His Spirit-empowered followers, has fueled and fired the growth of Christianity for two thousand years, and will continue to do so until "the end of the age."

As a Mom Heart group leader, you are part of that wildfire of faith. You're adding fuel to that fire when you respond to the "Great Commission" of Jesus by going to your world—your neighborhood, your church, your community, your city— to make disciples. Just like the apostles who spread Christ's teaching of the kingdom of God in *their* place and time, you are empowered by the Spirit of Christ within you to be a

> You are one of the "faithful people" that Paul envisioned teaching others to teach others. As a Mom Heart group leader and teacher, you have a message of inestimable value to give to the women in your group.

witness and worker for Jesus in *your* place and time. You "Go" because Jesus is with you, in you, empowering you by His Holy Spirit to be His witness in your little corner of the "remotest part of earth." No matter who you are, God wants to use you to make disciples.

Ask yourself the following questions about your ministry for Christ from the passages in Matthew and Acts:

- How does Christ's last command to "make disciples" apply to me, right here and right now? How can I be a disciple of Christ ready to make disciples?
- Where and when can I "go" to make disciples? Am I standing still, or moving forward for Jesus and His kingdom? What part of the world can I reach?
- How am I "teaching" disciples about Jesus and the things that He and His followers taught? How am I teaching them to guard all that Christ and His Word teach?
- Is Christ with me? Do I believe He is "always" with me, all the time and in every place? How does that make a difference in my life?
- Is the Holy Spirit within me? Do I believe that I receive "power" from Him? How does that make a difference in my life?
- Am I a witness for Christ? Do I believe that Jesus will use me to witness for Him right here and right now? How does that make a difference in my life?

## God Wants You to Teach Others What You Know
## 2 TIMOTHY 1:13–14, 2:1–2

The apostles knew what they were being sent out to do,

but how did Christianity grow so rapidly and spread so widely to become the largest religion in the world? The spiritual engine of growth for Christianity was in an uncomplicated principle of disciple-making that Jesus taught His disciples— teach others to teach others.

The growth of Christianity, though, is about more than just a methodology. Before anything else, it is about the message that inspires the method. Without the message of truth in God's Word, the method would be just religious activity. Listen to what Paul wanted Timothy to understand:

> Retain the standard of sound words which you have heard from me, in the faith and love which are in Christ Jesus. Guard, through the Holy Spirit who dwells in us, the treasure which has been entrusted to you. ... You therefore, my son, be strong in the grace that is in Christ Jesus. The things which you have heard from me in the presence of many witnesses, entrust these to faithful men who will be able to teach others also.
> (2 Timothy 1:13-14, 2:1-2)

Paul packs a lot into those few verses, exhorting Timothy to "retain" (hold onto) the truths he had heard, "guard" them as a "treasure," stay "strong" in Christ, and "entrust" the message to others he could trust. This was long before the new Scriptures that were still being written would become what we now know as the New Testament. In that first generation of Christianity, it all had to be truth invested in hearts and minds by faith.

In delivering his exhortations to Timothy, Paul touches on key words of the Christian message—faith (1:13), love (1:13), Christ Jesus (1:13, 2:1), Holy Spirit (1:14), grace (2:1), witnesses (2:2), faithful (2:2), teach (2:2), and others. These were not just "God words" in a final pep talk to Timothy; they were the life-changing language of hope and truth that opened hearts to the message of the gospel in all its fullness. They are powerful words that have changed the world, and should change you as a person, and as a Mom Heart group leader. It is a "treasure ... entrusted to you."

The incomparable message you have to teach and to share as a Mom Heart group leader is unlike any message ever shared in all of human history. It is the one true message that explains all other messages. You have the opportunity to open the pages of God's Word to the women in your group and draw them into the depths of His story and glory.

Timothy was one of the first links in the chain of "faithful men" (NASB) who would preserve the "treasure" of truth in the Bible that you now read, study, and teach. You are carrying on Paul's admonition to "entrust [what you have learned] to faithful men who will be able to teach others

> As a Mom Heart group leader, you have a "good work" to do. God wants to use you to help others grow in Him.

also." And just to clarify, Paul was not excluding you as a woman in his charge to Timothy. A better translation is: "entrust [what you have learned] to faithful people [*anthropois*] who will be competent to teach others as well" (NET).

That's you. You are one of the "faithful people" that Paul envisioned teaching others to teach others. As a Mom Heart group leader and teacher, you have a message of inestimable value to give to the women in your group. If you feel inadequate for that task, just know Paul felt the same way: "But we have this treasure in earthen vessels, so that the surpassing greatness of the power will be of God and not from ourselves" (2 Corinthians 4:5-7). As a fellow "earthen vessel," ask yourself the following questions to ponder your place in the process of passing on the truth of Scripture to other faithful followers, the same truth that Paul passed on to Timothy:

- How can I respond to Paul's admonitions to "retain," "guard," "be strong," and "entrust"? How am I, as one entrusted with the truths of God, preserving, promoting, and passing on that "treasure" to other faithful people?

> Faith is not always easy, life can become difficult, and we, too, can lose our confidence in Christ. That is why we dare not "forsake our assembling together."

- What can I do to make sure that I can "be strong in the grace that is in Christ Jesus"? What am I doing to strengthen my spirit with the grace of God? How am I opening my spirit to receive God's grace through the Word, prayer, and fellowship?

- How am I deliberately entrusting to other trustworthy women the truths that I know and am learning? How do I do that actively, and not just passively? How can I be strategic?

- How am I growing in my knowledge of the deep truths of Scripture revealed in Paul's words to Timothy? What other treasured words are doors into deeper understanding of all that God has done for us in Christ? What can I do to study these words?

## God Wants You to Learn and Teach the Scripture
## 2 TIMOTHY 3:14-17

Do you ever feel like you're not really qualified to teach anyone the Bible? The apostles probably felt that way at some point. They had relied entirely on Jesus' divine words and instruction for three years, and then He was gone. Jesus had taught "as one having authority" (Mark 1:22). How would these common, "uneducated and untrained men" (Acts 1:13) be able to pick up where Jesus left off?

If you feel that way, just remember that the apostles had no natural authority to teach others anything about God. But Jesus had taught them, and it was enough that each apostle became "like his teacher" (Luke 6:40). Their authority would be supernatural, coming from Jesus and the Holy Spirit and not from themselves (see John 15:26-27, 16:13-15). If you're following Jesus, and reading His Word to become like him, then you're walking in the same shoes as the apostles did. And don't miss the bigger truth: All of what the apostles had then to start the church, we have now collected in the thirty-nine books of the Old Testament and twenty-seven books of the New Testament. In your Bible, you have all you need to lead and teach with the authority of Christ.

The apostle Paul foresaw that the Scriptures would be all that followers of Jesus, then or in generations yet to come, would need in order to grow in Christ and become mature. Paul was in a Roman prison waiting to be martyred when he wrote his last letter to Timothy, his son in the faith and ministry protégé. He reminded Timothy not to worry that he (Paul) would soon be gone, but to continue to teach what he knew to be true:

> You, however, continue in the things you have learned and become convinced of, knowing from whom you have learned

them, and that from childhood you have known the sacred writings which are able to give you the wisdom that leads to salvation through faith which is in Christ Jesus. All Scripture is inspired by God and profitable for teaching, for reproof, for correction, for training in righteousness; so that the man of God may be adequate, equipped for every good work.
(2 Timothy 3:14-17)

Paul boldly declares that "all Scripture is inspired by God." It is not just a passive repository of inspiring information, but "God breathed" words that are useful and beneficial "for teaching, for reproof, for correction, for training righteousness." By God's design, its purpose is to make every person who is dedicated to Him adequate and capable to live for Him, "[fully] equipped for every good work" (see Ephesians 2:8-10). In the same spirit, Paul admonished Timothy earlier in the letter, "Be diligent to

> Just like those early Christians, we too are alone and far from home. Only the Word of God and the fellowship of other believers enables us to "hold fast the confession of our hope without wavering" (10:22).

present yourself approved to God as a workman who does not need to be ashamed, accurately handling the word of truth" (2:15). Scripture is the tool for whatever work we do for God.

As a Mom Heart group leader, you have a "good work" to do. God wants to use you to help others grow in Him. When you read the words "the man of God" in 2 Timothy 3:17, Paul meant you as a woman, too. The term for man, *anthropos*, is more accurately translated "the person dedicated to God" (NET). In other words, the power and purpose of Scripture is for every person, male and female. God has given Scripture not only to help you become mature, but also to make you capable and fitted to the work of ministry and fully equipped to help others become mature. Scripture, the Word of God, is the heart of your ministry as a Mom Heart group leader—it is the message God has equipped you to teach.

Ask yourself the following questions about your teaching ministry of the Word of God:

- What biblical truth and wisdom have I "learned and become convinced of" as I have followed Christ? What influence has Scripture had in my life since childhood? Who has influenced me as a believer?
- When reading the Scripture, am I reading words about God, or the God-breathed Word of God? How do others know that the Word of God is "living and active" when I teach?
- How have I profited from Scripture's teaching, reproof, correction, and training in righteousness? What specific benefits has it added to my life?
- As a "person dedicated to God" (NET), how has Scripture enabled and equipped me for life and for ministry to others? If my Mom Heart group is a "good work" that God has equipped me to do, is there any reason I should feel inadequate or unprepared to fulfill that ministry? How do I teach my group that Scripture can fully enable and equip them as well?

## God Wants You to Meet With and Encourage Others
### HEBREWS 10:22–25

Did you ever have to move away from a home where you'd lived a long time; a home you didn't want to leave? And when you got to your new home, at first all you could think about was what you missed, not what you now had that was new and full of possibility? Until you met a new friend who reminded you that it would get better, and encouraged you, and loved you. You were far from home and felt all alone, but that friend, and others you would make, helped you get through that transition.

The book of Hebrews was written to Jewish believers scattered by the persecution in Jerusalem after the stoning of Stephen. They left behind the temple, sacrifices, traditions, and familiar sights, sounds, and smells of Jerusalem that had made faith a tangible experience. Now they were being asked to live by the intangible beliefs of their new Christian faith—by the Holy Spirit within them, and by faith, hope, love, and grace. It was hard to believe in Jesus, and some wanted to return to the familiar and tangible security of "home" in Jerusalem. But the writer reminds them what they need to do when they're alone and far from home—to be faithful and to encourage one another:

> Let us hold fast the confession of our hope without wavering, for He who promised is faithful; and let us consider how to stimulate one another to love and good deeds, not forsaking our own assembling together, as is the habit of some, but encouraging one another; and all the more as you see the day drawing near. (Hebrews 10:23-25)

Just like those early Christians, we too are alone and far from home. Only the Word of God and the fellowship of other believers enables us to "hold fast the confession of our hope without wavering" (10:22). It's a long journey between here and

141

heaven, but God is with us and is faithful to His promises.

Faith is not always easy, life can become difficult, and we, too, can lose our confidence in Christ. That is why we dare not "forsake our assembling together" (10:25). We need each other; endurance is not meant to be a solo effort. Just a few verses later, the writer admonishes them, "Therefore, do not throw away your confidence, which has a great reward. For you have need of endurance so that when you have done the will of God, you may receive what was promised" (10:35-36). He's speaking to all of them; endurance is a group effort.

As a Mom Heart group leader and teacher, you are putting into practice what the writer of Hebrews told those early Christians they needed to do to be confident on the journey of faith. You are "assembling together" to "hold fast the confession of our hope" and to "stimulate one another to love and good deeds" so that you all can be women known for "encouraging one another" as you live your lives together for Christ. Ask yourself the following questions to help you press in and press on in your vital, biblical ministry to women:

- How can I "hold fast the confession" of all that I hope for in Christ? What can cause me to be "wavering" about that hope? What will help me be strong in faith?

- What "promises of God" strengthen my faith and steady my hope? How have I seen God be "faithful" to me and my family?

- How can I lead and tend my Mom Heart group so that we "stimulate one another to love and good deeds"? How can I make sure that we are "encouraging one another" every time we are together?

- Is there anything that could make me want to "throw away [my] confidence" in Christ? How can I protect against that in the times when I "have need of endurance" so that I will be able to do the will of God.

## What Do You Want to Do for God?

Leading and teaching a Mom Heart group is not about authority, or great faith, or special training, or strong personality, or spiritual giftedness, or appearance, or deep knowledge. It's about being faithful to serve, available to God, and willing to learn. David, who would become king of Israel, did not look like a future king, but God told Samuel to choose

> If you're ready to become a link in the 2,000-year-old chain stretching back to Jesus, Paul, and Timothy, and all who have followed them, then take that step of faith.

and anoint him, "for man looks at the outward appearance, but the LORD looks at the heart" (1 Samuel 16:7). If you are faithful, available, and teachable, then God is not concerned about the outward appearances such as worldly qualifications and qualities; God is looking at your heart. "For the eyes of the LORD move to and fro throughout the earth that He may strongly support those whose heart is completely His" (2 Chronicles 16:9).

If you have read this far, then it seems likely that God is working in your heart. If you believe there is a need today to "restore moms' hearts to God's heart for motherhood," then perhaps God is moving you to start a Mom Heart group. You can pray, get counsel from others, research, and make Pro-

Con lists, but in the end you will need to take a step of faith. At some point you will say to God, "I believe this is what you want me to do, so I am ready to take a step of faith and do it." That's when you move from walking by sight, to walking by faith (2 Corinthians 5:7)–that's when you say, "This is what I want to do for God."

If you're ready to become a link in the 2,000-year-old chain stretching back to Jesus, Paul, Timothy, and all who have followed them, then take that step of faith. You will be blessed because of your faith, and other moms will be blessed through you.

# HINTS: THE METHODS

## Faithfully Following the Footsteps

» **Discipleness:** Every Christian is a disciple. In the gospels, the term is often used simply to describe those who were following Jesus. However, not every Christian is a "faithful disciple." Jesus calls His followers to be more than DINOs, or "disciples in name only." He wants followers who will be faithful to His cause. We call that quality "discipleness." You grow in discipleness by growing closer to Jesus–hearing His heart, understanding His mission, and taking up His cross to follow. Read through the gospels and take time to meditate and journal on the passages and parables where Jesus describes the qualities and character of a disciple that He is looking for in faithful followers.

In the same way you want to grow in godliness as a leader of others, you can also grow in discipleness as a follower of Jesus.

» **Teaching:** It is not uncommon for someone to excuse themselves from ministry by saying, "I just don't have the gift of teaching." Yes, teaching is a gift of the Spirit, but the gift is not required of every teacher. An elder of the church, the highest office of leadership, is required only to be "able to teach" (1 Timothy 3:2), not to have the spiritual gift of teaching. In other words, teaching is a leadership skill that can be learned and improved. As a leader of other women, you can grow in your ability to teach. Seek out good books on teaching, listen to messages on audio or video, and meet with other teachers in your church or community to help one another be better teachers. You may have wonderful insights to teach others, but your teaching skills will either hinder or help you to communicate them well to others. Whether you have the gift of teaching or not, choose to become a skilled teacher. You can do it.

» **Togethering:** The maxim is probably true that success in life often comes from just showing up, but it goes a step further for Christian ministry. Success in ministry often comes from just getting together. The exhortation in Hebrews to "encourage one another" requires a group of more than one Christian. When you bring others together, you are creating the opportunity for real ministry to happen. It won't happen unless someone first initiates. You don't have to have it all together to get others together. Just do it.

» **Grow Into It:** Becoming a faithful disciple who ministers to others does not happen overnight. Take your time to become comfortable with the methods of ministry discussed in this chapter, and in this book, and simply grow into them. The more you step out in faith and do the ministry, the more you will "grow up in all aspects into Him who is the head, even Christ" (Ephesians 4:15).

» **Resources:** Treat your ministry the same way you would any other important responsibility or task you are given as a Christian—"Whatever you do in word or deed, do all in the name of the Lord Jesus ..." (Colossians 3:17). In other words, do it in a way that will honor Christ. Part of that will be wanting to grow and be better at the task God has given you to do. So, begin building up a library of resources, whether physical or digital, to help you as a teacher and group leader. Consider them the tools you need to do your ministry "in the name of the Lord Jesus" well.

# Notes

_____

_____

_____

_____

_____

_____

_____

_____

_____

_____

_____

_____

_____

_____

_____

_____

_____

_____

_____

_____

# Section 10
# THE MATERIALS

**There is a Word of God because we were created by a God of words.** We need verbal words because God designed us to communicate, interact, relate, inform, discuss, and persuade one another verbally. But we also need written words because God designed us to read, learn, understand, grow, remember, and witness from all that he has revealed and written in the Scriptures. Because we are created to read his Word, we are also created to read the words of others in books, resources, and materials. Printed materials are the lifeblood of a Mom Heart group.

The spiritual life at home is a practice of living, a way of seeing, and a habit of prayer that sets God and his kingdom at the center of all you teach and do. ... Home can be one of the most deeply transformative places in the world, a refuge where hearts are shaped and God is known. ... It's in your home and presence that your children will learn what it means to be a follower of Christ.

~ *10 Gifts of Wisdom,* Sally Clarkson

# TENDING YOUR MOM HEART GROUP

All it really takes to start a Mom Heart group is some moms with open hearts and open Bibles. However, you'll likely want more than that to help you keep your group growing, and to go deeper as mothers who are seeking after God's heart. That's where other thoughtful and relevant books, materials, and resources come into the picture—tools to help you dig deeper into the Word, think clearly about biblical motherhood, influence others, and to build a strong group.

Our vision for Mom Heart is about building people, not building an organization. It has never been our intent to conceive and control the content of every Mom Heart group. Rather, our intent has always been to encourage, equip, and enable mom-hearted mothers to minister to other moms. It's not about becoming a bigger ministry, but about becoming better ministers. It's all about inspiring you, training you, and giving you the tools you need to accomplish three basic tasks of being a Mom Heart group leader:

**Starting:** Getting Your Group Going

**Leading:** Giving Your Group Direction

**Tending:** Growing Your Group Personally

If we can help you be confident and fruitful in those three tasks, then we know God will be faithful to take it from there. The resources listed on the following pages are books, materials, and media we have written, created, and published for Whole Heart Ministries and Mom Heart Ministry. It will always be an incomplete list, but it is always completely sufficient to equip you for ministry. Most of the materials are available on MomHeart.com or on WholeHeart.org in the Whole Heart Store.

# Mom Heart Resources

## Print Books

*The Mission of Motherhood*, Sally Clarkson — Sally's foundational book about God's biblical design and heart for motherhood. Recommended for new groups.

*The Ministry of Motherhood*, Sally Clarkson — Sally's follow-up book about following the example of Jesus' relationship with His disciples in mothering.

*Seasons of a Mother's Heart*, Sally Clarkson — Essays on motherhood for Christian and homeschooling mothers. Extensive Bible study and discussion questions.

*The Mom Walk*, Sally Clarkson — An exploration of what it means to walk with God as a mother. Personal stories, biblical insights, discussion questions.

*Dancing with My Father*, Sally Clarkson – Personal and biblical insights on how you can live with joy and grace as a woman, wife, and mother even when life is difficult.

*Desperate: Hope for the Mom Who Needs to Breathe*, Sarah Mae and Sally Clarkson – Encouragement and hope for young moms struggling under the burdens of motherhood.

*You Are Loved*, Sally Clarkson and Angela Perritt – An eight-week guided Bible study with commentary on "embracing the everlasting love God has for you."

*Own Your Life*, Sally Clarkson – A personal, biblical, and motivational call to Christian women to "own" the life, opportunities, and ministry God has given to them.

*10 Gifts of Wisdom*, Sally Clarkson – Biblical and practical insights about ten qualities of wisdom to build into your children before they leave your home.

*10 Gifts of Grace **, Sally and Clay Clarkson – Biblical and practical insights for parents on creating a grace-shaped home to instill ten grace messages in children's hearts.

*10 Gifts of Truth **, Clay Clarkson – Biblical and practical insights on ten key biblical truths that your children need to know and understand before they leave home.

*Heartfelt Discipline*, Clay Clarkson – A deeply biblical examination of childhood discipline with a new "path of life" model for leading your children to walk with God.

*Our 24 Family Ways*, Clay Clarkson – A family devotional and discipleship guide based on 24 expressions of biblical family values, with 120 devotions and much more.

*Educating the WholeHearted Child*, Clay Clarkson (with Sally Clarkson) – If you lead a group for homeschooling moms, this 384-page book is full of useful material.

## E-books

Most of our print books are also available as ebooks.

Check MomHeart.com and WholeHeart.org regularly for new ebook releases.

## Media

The media below can be found on MomHeart.com, WholeHeart.org, SallyClarkson.com, YouTube.com, or Vimeo.com.

**Mom Heart-Beats video** – Short (8-12 minutes) video introductions to selected books by Sally, with personal comments about each chapter.

**Mom Heart Conference audio** – Sally's messages, and others, from WholeHearted Mother and Mom Heart Conferences, 1998-present.

**WholeHearted Child Home Education Workshop audio** – Sally's original homeschooling workshop audio from 1996 and 1997.

**WholeHearted Learning audio** * – Clay and Sally on their homeschooling model on the 20th anniversary of *Educating the WholeHearted Child.*

**Mom Heart Webinar videos** * – Video recordings of Sally's live webinars on a variety of topics for Christian women, wives, and mothers.

**Whole Heart Webinar videos** * – Video recordings of Christian home and parenting webinars with Sally, Clay, Sarah, and others.

**Mom Heart Group Leader Training audio/video** * – Audio and video recordings of Sally and others training Mom Heart group leaders.

**Life-Giving Words with Sally podcasts \*** – Audio clips and messages by Sally on a variety of topics for life-giving mothers and women.

## Online

**MomHeart.com** – Articles, audio, and video designed to encourage you as a mother, and to equip you to start, lead, and tend a Mom Heart group.

**SallyClarkson.com** – Sally's personal blog for Christian women and mothers since 2007. Inspirational, biblical, and insightful posts by Sally.

**MomHeartConference.com** – Since 1998, an annual hotel weekend winter getaway for Christian moms with Sally and guests.

**WholeHeart.org** – Whole Heart Online provides information about Whole Heart Ministries, books and resources, and other helps for Christian families.

**Storyformed.com** – A new ministry initiative of Whole Heart led by Sarah Clarkson to explore books, story, and imagination in family life and child development.

**HeartfeltDiscipline.com \*** – Clay Clarkson's blog to define, discuss, debate, and defend biblical discipline and training of children based on his book.

## Social Media

Sally is connected through Facebook, Twitter, Pinterest, and YouTube through several pages and channels.

\* Limited availability or a planned future release

# MOM HEART MINISTRY
# GUIDING DOCUMENTS

Every movement of God is like a train. In order for it to move it must have two things: (1) it needs fuel for its engine, and (2) it needs tracks to run on. We've defined our ministry vision in this book—where we want the train of this movement to go. But a train needs fuel and tracks to get to where it is going—our ministry values are the fuel and our ministry beliefs are the tracks. When the engine is fired up with the fuel of our values, and the wheels are running along the tracks of our beliefs, there will be movement toward our vision. Every Christian movement is defined by its vision, values, and beliefs.

Our vision for Mom Heart is not to build an organization to manage, but to release a movement of mothers to minister to other mothers. Our role is simply to encourage, equip, and enable them to "restore moms' hearts to God's heart for motherhood." To keep the Mom Heart movement from losing steam or going off the rails, though, we ask only that each Mom Heart group leader be able to wholeheartedly affirm our vision, values, and beliefs. That is the purpose of this book and the two documents that follow.

## What Is Our "Ministry Values Statement"?

The term "covenant" may sound a little formal or serious to you, but it is really just a way to say, "I agree. I'm on board." Our "Ministry Values Statement" is an informal covenant. It's not a law and we don't require you to sign something to prove your loyalty; it is simply our effort to ensure that a group that takes the name "Mom Heart" will, at its heart, be known for certain biblical and sensible qualities. If you believe God is directing you to become a Mom Heart group leader, then we ask only that you carefully and prayerfully read the statement and decide if what we are trying to build is something you can wholeheartedly support. If it is, then we are here to encourage, equip, and enable you to join us in this movement. If you are on board this train, then God can use you to change the world one mom heart at-a-time.

## What Is Our "Ministry Beliefs Statement"?

"If you don't stand for something you'll fall for anything." The early church might not have produced such a pithy and clever maxim, but they certainly believed its proverbial truth, as witnessed and preserved in statements of faith such as the Apostles' and Nicene creeds. Following the Protestant Reformation in 1517, every subsequent expression of the church needed its own statement of faith to differentiate itself from all the other expressions of the church. Today, a typical statement of faith serves two general purposes: (1) to affirm orthodox biblical beliefs, and (2) to express distinctive biblical beliefs. In the denominational era, it's less about standing for something so you don't fall into error, and more about, "You can't tell the players without a scorecard." Our "Ministry Beliefs Statement" aims at two goals: (1) to align with historic Christian belief, and (2) to express core beliefs that shape the Mom Heart vision and message.

## Why Does Mom Heart Need These Documents?

We want the words "Mom Heart" to mean some very specific things, but we also want them to <u>not</u> mean some other things. Our "Ministry Beliefs Statement" is not a detailed and comprehensive document for a reason: We want to include mothers from as many church and theological traditions as we possibly can. However, that creates doctrinal gaps that others can fill in with their own theological beliefs. So, our "Ministry Values Statement" attempts to resolve that problem: We want to define some reasonable biblical boundaries to limit what can be added to the gaps. If you want to be a Mom Heart group leader, we simply ask that you affirm and embrace the things that make us Mom Heart, as expressed in these two documents.

# MINISTRY VALUES STATEMENT

## Our Vision

Mom Heart Ministry is a Christian movement and informal network of small groups for mothers that seeks to restore moms' hearts to God's heart for motherhood. We believe God's eternal purpose for mothers was evident at creation in His design for marriage and the family. Our vision is to encourage, equip, and enable mothers to start, lead, and tend Mom Heart groups around the world. We affirm and embrace the values in this document:

## Our Values

**We value GOD'S WORD, not opinions.** – A Mom Heart leader keeps group discussion grounded in what the Bible says, in historical and biblical context, to us today. She does not allow herself or others to promote or defend favored experts or personal opinions that can constrain others from participation.

**We value CHRIST, not theologies.** – A Mom Heart leader keeps group discussion focused ultimately on the person and work of Christ. She does not allow herself or others to promote or defend systematic theologies, personal dogmas, church traditions, or controversial views that can divide and exclude.

**We value LOVE, not expectations.** – A Mom Heart leader keeps group discussion focused on expressing love and acceptance of one another. She does not allow herself or others to add extra-biblical expectations or conditions to the love and forgiveness of Christ offered unconditionally in His gospel.

**We value GRACE, not laws.** – A Mom Heart leader keeps group attitudes focused on our grace and freedom in Christ. She does not allow herself or others to express Christian laws and rules that create a burden of guilt by requiring works or specific beliefs of any kind not specifically required in Scripture.

**We value SPIRIT, not control.** – A Mom Heart leader keeps group life and activities focused on listening and responding to the Holy Spirit's direction. She does not allow herself or others to impose formal requirements more concerned about control and order than about the Holy Spirit's leading in the group.

**We value PEOPLE, not tasks.** – A Mom Heart leader keeps group life and activities focused on the needs of people made in God's image and loved by Him. She does not allow herself or others to let the accomplishing of tasks and projects distract from or displace a sensitivity to the people being served.

**We value MINISTRY, not exclusion.** – A Mom Heart leader keeps group life and activities focused on loving and serving others inside and outside the group. She does not allow herself or others to become comfortable, complacent, and cliquish, but looks for ways to reach out, serve, and include others.

# MINISTRY BELIEFS STATEMENT

## What Mom Heart Believes

Mom Heart Ministry is a small groups and teaching initiative of Whole Heart Ministries, a nonprofit (501c3) Christian organization. Whole Heart Ministries adheres to the Statement of Faith of the National Association of Evangelicals (NAE). The "Ministry Beliefs Statement" that follows is a summarized and narrative expression of the core biblical beliefs that define and direct the Mom Heart Ministry initiative. We affirm and embrace the beliefs in this document:

## Mom Heart Ministry Beliefs Statement

**WORD:** We affirm the entire Bible, both the Old and New Testaments as they have been faithfully transmitted and accurately translated, as God's complete, true, and trustworthy Word–His finished and inspired revelation to all people, our sole authority in matters of spiritual truth concerning God and mankind, and our trustworthy guide in all matters of salvation, life, faith, and godliness.

**JESUS:** We affirm the essential doctrines of God's Word recognized and accepted as the historic and orthodox Christian faith, and the centrality of the person and work of Jesus Christ to that faith–His divine-human nature, virgin birth, sinless life, attesting miracles, atoning death, bodily resurrection, ascension into heaven, present spiritual kingdom rule and reign, and future return in glory.

**CROSS:** We affirm that Christ died on the cross as a vicarious, substitutionary sacrifice to atone for the sin of all mankind, and that the life in His blood removed our guilt and reconciled us to God by satisfying God's justice and appeasing His wrath—the mystery of the cross demonstrates the grace that "God so loved the world" and the victory that Christ won over the powers of evil for mankind.

**GRACE:** We affirm for all who come to Jesus in faith that "by grace you have been saved through faith; and that not of yourselves, it is the gift of God" because "grace and truth were realized through Jesus Christ" to set us free from the demands of the Law and of works so that "there is now no condemnation for those who are in Christ Jesus"—faith alone is the way to God's salvation by grace.

**MARRIAGE:** We affirm the biblical design for marriage as one man and one woman, united spiritually and physically for life, becoming as one for the purposes of fulfilling God's creation mandate to bear children and to subdue and rule over creation, and for presenting to the world a living picture of the relationship of Christ and His church by serving God together with mutual love and respect.

**FAMILY:** We affirm the biblical design for the family, blessed by God "in the beginning," for passing faith from one generation to the next, for training and instructing children in the Lord who will honor their parents and fear and follow God, for affirming that every child is a blessing and gift of God to be welcomed and desired, and for picturing the nature and character of the invisible God.

**CHURCH:** We affirm the biblical priority of the church, which is the visible body of Christ in both its local and universal expressions, in defending and extending the faith entrusted to it, and the absolute necessity of the work of God's Holy Spirit, both in the world and in the believer, for enabling individual Christians to live according to that faith and to grow in godly character and obedience.

# Mom Heart Group
# Planning Forms

There is no one way to plan for a group meeting. Some moms can do it all in their heads on the go, others do it all ahead of time on paper. Sides can be taken on the matter, but neither way is right or wrong. Our observation is that individual planning style is mostly a matter of personality type and preference, tempered by past training and experience. Whatever your planning style may be, though, the familiar axiom will always be true: If you fail to plan, you plan to fail. You should be careful not to under-plan or to over-plan, but you should always be committed to adequately plan.

The Mom Heart group planning forms that we provide are resources you can use if they will be helpful. The forms shown in this book are available as full sized (8.5"x11") PDFs on MomHeart.com as free downloads. As the movement and the MomHeart.com website grow, you may find other helpful forms there as well. If you happen to enjoy creating a well-designed form, then generate a PDF of your creation and email it to us and we'll consider adding it to the collection online. The planning forms currently available include:

**Mom Heart Ministry Action Plan (MAP)** – This two-page form will guide you through the process of identifying the purpose for your group, and determining what will be needed or required of you in order to start, lead, and tend your group effectively.

**Mom Heart Group Planning Sheet (GPS)** – This two-page form provides a quick and easy way to plan your Mom Heart group meetings or other events. It will help you to insure that everything needed for a good meeting is taken care of or delegated.

**Mom Heart Group Lesson Planner (GLP)** – This two-page form will walk you through creating your own Mom Heart group HEART lesson plan. It will help you to create a clear roadmap for leading your group in a meaningful Bible study and discussion.

**Mom Heart Group Member Information (GMI)** – This one-page form will help you keep track of each of your Mom Heart group members with contact information, family details, important dates, interests and involvements, special needs, and hobbies.

The forms on the following pages are reduced images of the full-size (8 ½" x 11") forms that are available on MomHeart.com as PDF files. These images are provided only to give you an idea for how to use the forms. You can also use the content from these forms as guides to organize your planning using other media.

# Mom Heart Ministry Action Plan (MAP)

| Prepared by: | Date: | Page 1 |
|---|---|---|

### — PRAY —

### — PURPOSE —

Vision — Why do you want to lead a Mom Heart group?

Purpose Statement — Why will your group meet?

### — PLAN —

Who will participate?

What will you study?

When will you meet?

Where will you meet?

How will you manage the group?

How many do you anticipate?

**Section 10: The Materials**

# Mom Heart Ministry Action Plan (MAP)

| Prepared by: | Date: | Page 2 |
| --- | --- | --- |

— PLAN (Calendar) —

Important dates and deadlines:

— PROMOTE —

Printed materials needed:

Online and social media to create:

Friends to contact:

Leaders to contact:

— PERSONAL NOTES —

# Mom Heart Group Planning Sheet (GPS)

| Day & Date: | Begin & End: | Page 1 |
|---|---|---|

## — DETAILS —

| | |
|---|---|
| Name of Group: | |
| Group Meeting Times: | |
| Current Book/Study: | |

## — CONTACTS —

| Location: | Arrive by: |
|---|---|
| Directions: | |
| Hostess: | |
| Phone: | Email: |
| Helper: | |
| Phone: | Email: |

## — PLANNING —

**Refreshments**

**Materials**

**Hospitality**

**Child Care**

**Lesson**

# Mom Heart Group Planning Sheet (GPS)

| Day & Date: | Begin & End: | Page 2 |

— CHECKLIST —

| ! | ✓ | # | Getting It Done | Do By |
|---|---|---|-----------------|-------|
| | | | | |
| | | | | |
| | | | | |
| | | | | |
| | | | | |
| | | | | |
| | | | | |
| | | | | |
| | | | | |
| | | | | |
| | | | | |
| | | | | |
| | | | | |
| | | | | |
| | | | | |
| | | | | |
| | | | | |
| | | | | |
| | | | | |
| | | | | |
| | | | | |

— NOTES —

| # | Memos to Self |
|---|---------------|
| | |
| | |
| | |
| | |
| | |
| | |
| | |
| | |
| | |

# Mom Heart Group Lesson Planner (HEART)

| Day & Date: | Lesson#: | Page 1 |
|---|---|---|

## — DETAILS —

| | |
|---|---|
| Lesson Title: | |
| Current Book/Study: | |
| Reading Assignment: | |
| Location: | |
| Notes: | |

### HEART — HEAR THE SPIRIT: Invitation — 10 minutes

| # | Discussion Questions / Notes (What is the Bible talking about?) |
|---|---|
| | |
| | |
| | |
| | |
| | |
| | |
| | |
| | |

### hEART — ENGAGE THE WORD: Observation — 45 minutes

| # | Scripture Passages / Notes (What does the Bible say?) |
|---|---|
| | |
| | |
| | |
| | |
| | |
| | |
| | |
| | |
| | |
| | |
| | |
| | |
| | |
| | |
| | |
| | |
| | |

# Mom Heart Group Lesson Planner (HEART)

| Day & Date: | Lesson#: | Page 2 |
|---|---|---|

HE**A**RT — AFFIRM THE TRUTH: Interpretation — **15** minutes

Questions to Ask / Notes (What does the Bible mean?)

Is there something God wants me to KNOW?

Is there something God wants me to BE?

Is there something God wants me to DO?

Is there something God wants me to BELIEVE?

What is the BIG IDEA?

> Subject: What did the lesson talk about?

> Complement: What did the lesson say about what we talked about?

> State the Big Idea of the lesson (Subject + Complement):

HEA**R**T — RESPOND TO GOD: Application — **5** minutes

Personal Reflections (What does the Bible mean to me?)

HEAR**T** — TAKE IT TO HEART: Supplication — **15** minutes

Prayer Requests (What does the Bible mean to us?)

Prayer requests recorder:

Special prayer needs:

170

# Mom Heart Group Member Info Sheet

| Name: | Nickname: |
|---|---|

## — CONTACT INFO —

| Home Address: | |
|---|---|
| Home Phone: | Message OK:   Y   N   ? |
| Mobile Phone: | Text/VM OK:   Y   N   ? |
| Work Phone: | Call OK:   Y   N   ? |
| Work Address: | |
| Personal Email: | |

## — FAMILY INFO —

| Name | Birthday | Age |
|---|---|---|
| Spouse: | | |
| Child: | | |
| Child: | | |
| Child: | | |
| Child: | | |
| Child: | | |
| Child: | | |
| Child: | | |
| Child: | | |

## — PROFILE INFO —

| | |
|---|---|
| Birthday: | Anniversary: |
| Church: | Ministry: |
| Preferred Bible Versions: | |
| Spiritual Gift(s): | |
| Hobbies: | |
| Activities: | |
| Family Occupation(s): | |
| Fav Stores: | |
| Fav Eateries: | |
| Fav Foods: | |
| Fav Beverages: | |
| Fav Music/Artists: | |
| Fav Books/Authors: | |
| Fav Movies/Actors: | |
| Other: | |

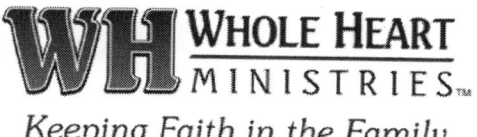

### WHOLE HEART
### MINISTRIES™

*Keeping Faith in the Family*

**Whole Heart Ministries** is a Christian home and parenting ministry founded by Clay and Sally Clarkson in 1994. Its mission is to encourage and equip Christian parents to raise wholehearted children for Christ. It offers quality books, events, media, and online resources to help parents. WholeHeart.org offers a Christian home and parenting blog and an online store with selected parenting resources. Whole Heart Ministries is a nonprofit, federally tax-exempt (501c3), evangelical Christian ministry. Mom Heart Ministry is a strategic ministry initiative of Whole Heart Ministries. For more information contact us at:

Whole Heart Ministries
P.O. Box 3445 • Monument, CO 80132
719-488-4466 • 888-488-4466
whm@wholeheart.org • www.wholeheart.org

## OUR BOOKS

Our books are available from the Whole Heart Store on WholeHeart.org and MomHeart.com, on Amazon.com, and from other quality booksellers. Look for our books by the following publishers:

Whole Heart Press
Apologia Press
WaterBrook Press
Thomas Nelson
Tyndale Publishers
Home for Good Book

Made in the USA
Middletown, DE
28 October 2016